IT'S YOUR
TURN

How to Rediscover Yourself
Prioritize Your Well-Being
& Thrive With Purpose

SHARI BIERY

It's Your Turn: How to Rediscover Yourself Prioritize Your Well-Being & Thrive with Purpose
Published by Alive With Purpose Publishing
Gulf Breeze, Florida, U.S.A.

Disclaimer: The information in this book is based on the author's own experiences and opinions. It is intended to provide helpful and informative material on the subject matter. The author and publisher are not liable for any damages or negative consequences resulting from the use of the information in this book.

BIERY, SHARI, Author
IT'S YOUR TURN
SHARI BIERY

Library of Congress Control Number: 2024926882

ISBN: 979-8-9916214-1-0, 979-8-9916214-3-4 (paperback)
ISBN: 979-8-9916214-0-3, 979-8-9916214-4-1 (hardcover)
ISBN: 979-8-9916214-2-7 (digital)

HEALTH & FITNESS / Women's Health
BODY, MIND & SPIRIT / Inspiration & Personal Growth
FAMILY & RELATIONSHIPS / Military Families

Book Cover & Graphic Design: Kristine Barrett, TimeTo Social Media, LLC
Brand Design: Michelle Griffin, Stand Out Women Media
Editing: Lezlee Alexander, LMA Services
Design & Production: Devon Whitney, Whitney Tech Support

QUANTITY PURCHASES: Schools, companies, professional groups, clubs, and other organizations may qualify for special terms when ordering quantities of this title. For information, email alivewithpurposecoaching@gmail.com

Self-care is giving the world the best of you,
instead of what's left of you.
—Katie Reed

Praise For It's Your Turn

"Shari's innate passion and genuine commitment to guiding women toward becoming their best selves shines through every page of *It's Your Turn*. Through Shari's insightful guidance, readers are empowered to view life's challenges not as setbacks, but as opportunities for growth. She delves into the profound realization that our responses, beliefs, and habits are learned, offering a roadmap for transforming mindsets surrounding various aspects of life, from money and self-worth to success and health habits. With unwavering positivity and ongoing encouragement, Shari skillfully peels back the layers of limitation, enabling readers to break free from what holds them back and to embrace their true potential. Her authentic sincerity and dedication to fostering positive change make her book a must read for anyone seeking to create a fulfilling and empowered life journey."

—Kristine Barrett, CEO, RN,
TimeTo Social Media LLC

"Shari Biery has written a must-read guide for any woman feeling like stress has gotten the best of us Read this book; learn the C.A.L.M. method of coming home to yourself again."

—Christine Williams, founder of Activate Abundance Academy and owner of Shine Wellness LLC,
https://shineabundancenow.com

"*It's Your Turn* is a must read for anyone who has put their dreams in the back seat out of service to others. After hard-won wisdom from service as a military spouse, Biery's proven, compassionate, and empowering roadmap will lead you to (re)discover your purpose, passion, and vitality—to bring out your ultimate gifts to the world while still loving the important people in your life. If you picked up this book, it's a sign that's it's your time, YOUR TURN!"

—Sara Connell, bestselling author of
The Science of Getting Rich for Women & founder of
Thought Leader Academy, https://www.saraconnell.com

"In *It's Your Turn,* Shari Biery is the heartfelt, compassionate, and whip-smart friend and expert you need as a midlife woman navigating your next phase. Her personal stories will move you and hit you hard as you recognize your own inner calling for direction and meaning. As a Purpose and Well-being Mentor, National Board Certified Health and Wellness Coach, and dedicated military spouse, Shari understands us, knows us, and lights the way to midlife inner renewal and purpose. Her C.A.L.M. Method is exactly that—a soothing yet strategic roadmap guiding you to a life where you and your desires matter. Whether you're a spouse of a partner with a high-achieving career or looking to redefine your next chapter, this book is your permission slip to start prioritizing yourself with an 'It's My Turn' mantra for a future embossed with confidence, health, and joy."

—Michelle B Griffin, author, speaker, and founder of
Standout Women Media, the thought leadership platform
for women experts, MichelleBGriffin.com

"Shari is as good a mentor as she is a friend, and in this book, you get both. She will meet you where you are, earn your trust, and lovingly lead you to a life that nourishes you as well as the people around you. Shari speaks with authenticity; she's been there, and she has receipts. She knows that the way out of chaos is not hustle and endless striving but in slowing down, simplifying, and tuning in to your inner guide. I recommend *It's Your Turn* to every woman who has put her purpose on the back burner and needs help finding her way back to herself. Shari is uniquely qualified to lead you on this journey."

—Lisa Deck, LCSW, founder of Embody Collective,
www.embodycollective.com

"Through engaging, beautifully written, true stories, author and former United States Navy wife, Shari Biery, strongly and lovingly encourages readers to place themselves first rather than last on their daily priority lists in order to live their best lives. Exercises are also offered at the end of each chapter to inspire real change towards better self-care, emotionally and physically. I have met Shari Biery and have engaged in multiple conversations with this astute author and coach. All I can say is, 'Thank you for your service in and out of the military and YES, Ma'am, forward march towards greater C.A.L.M.!'"

—Marjie Hadad, speaker and author,
The Power of PR Parenting: How to Raise Confident,
Resilient, and Successful Children Using
Public Relations Strategies

"After diving into *It's Your Turn*, my life was a whirlwind of constant hustle and pushing. Raised with the notion that rest is for the weak, I lived by the motto, 'you can sleep when you're dead.' However, Shari's wisdom shifted my perspective entirely. She enlightened me on the importance of rest as a crucial factor in generating revenue. Learning to prioritize myself daily was a game-changer; previously, I wore exhaustion and self-sacrifice as badges of honor. Now, I understand that clarity is unattainable amidst chaos. This book is essential reading for any woman experiencing compassion fatigue."

—Molly McGrath,
Hiring & Empowering Solutions, LLC,
www.hiringandempowering.com

"Shari Biery's words will hit home for every military spouse leaving active duty military life. It speaks directly to rediscovering who you are and insight into how to move forward with confidence. This book is a must-read for all transitioning spouses."

—Anna Larson, Founder, MilSpouse Transition,
www.milspousetransition.com

Table of Contents

This book is dedicated to the incredible military and service spouses—the unsung heroes—who bring strength and love to the home front. Your visible and invisible sacrifices create a sense of stability and love for an entire nation.

You embody courage and grace in facing some of the most difficult challenges.

Yet, you still keep sharing your gifts of the heart.

Medical And Mental Health Disclaimer

The information provided in this book is intended for educational and informational purposes only. It is not a substitute for professional medical, mental health, and/or psychological advice, diagnosis, or treatment. Always seek the advice of your physician or other qualified health and mental health providers with any questions you may have regarding a medical condition. Never disregard professional medical advice or delay in seeking it because of something you have read in this book.

Privacy Disclaimer

To protect my clients' privacy, I have changed their names and identifying details in the stories shared in this book. While real experiences inspire these stories, any resemblance to actual persons, living or dead, or actual events is purely coincidental. I deeply respect the confidentiality and trust of my clients, and their privacy is of the utmost importance.

Introduction

There was a time in my life when exhaustion had taken over, leaving me searching for answers. Sitting in my car after a doctor's appointment, I pondered the unanswered questions lingering within me. Struggling with night sweats, insomnia, weight gain, and fatigue were the physical symptoms. Armed with a prescription that promised relief but left me questioning if it was the solution to the deeper issues I faced. It was a turbulent period marked by feelings of resentment, a search for purpose, changing identities, self-sacrifice, and a sense of unworthiness, all while navigating the challenges of being a woman in the transition of midlife.

Why was I feeling this way, and could a single prescription truly address the complexities of what was going on with me? It was a question that propelled me on a journey in search of profound answers and a genuine understanding of the challenges that had taken over my well-being. After years of making sacrifices, I searched for a resource to guide me through the emotions and uncertainties I faced. I have always been a strong woman, but even strong people can feel isolated. I longed for connection and community but found it challenging to express what was happening within me.

In the quest for answers, I needed a different approach to my self-care, not just one more thing to add to my to-do list. A new way of embracing who I was and a way of integrating self-care into my daily existence. This journey became an exploration of how to cultivate a lifestyle where taking care of myself wasn't just a task but a part of everyday life.

This book was born from that search for answers. Exploring desires often left unspoken, tucked away in the quiet recesses of my heart. Like you, I've felt the yearning for something undefined—a desire for purpose echoing in the depths of my soul. I felt lost and didn't know where to turn for answers. I no longer recognized the woman in the mirror. I had lost the brightness and inner glow. I felt a disconnection from myself that was hard to describe. Perhaps you've hesitated to share these feelings too, fearing that no one would understand or doubting whether it's worth expressing.

As I was writing this book, I scrolled through a Facebook group for military spouses. I was amazed at how accurately one woman expressed what I had gone through. The anonymous military spouse shared the struggle of feeling like she was losing herself. The painful experience of giving away pieces of herself, sacrificing a career for a spouse, surrendering her body for her children, and relinquishing the once-enjoyed hobbies due to the time-consuming nature of military life. Her haunting words, "I no longer recognize the woman staring back at me in the mirror. I feel like a distant second in this partnership," struck a nerve. The feeling of being relegated to a supportive role was familiar.

The post shared a narrative of the challenges many military spouses face. Hundreds of women responded to the post with a simple yet profound "me too," revealing a common thread of emotions and struggles. This silent solidarity speaks volumes about the mutual challenges many women face. This anonymous post sheds light on the fear and hesitation often accompanying women expressing genuine feelings. The collective acknowledgment underscores the importance of providing a space for women to be authentic and connect over their shared experiences, fostering a sense of understanding and support.

Through the pages ahead, I draw from my experiences and lessons learned as a wife, mom, military spouse, and now a National Board Certified Health and Wellness Coach (NBC-HWC). Some solutions were found in the medical community, but many surfaced elsewhere. I realized I had to be my own advocate because no one was looking out for my best interests but me. We may be focused on caring for everyone else, but the time is now to take ownership of our well-being and know we are worthy of it. No one is coming to save us. We have to save ourselves.

You may be wondering how or where to even start. That's why I am committed to honestly sharing what influenced my path to wellness and the growth that emerged from it. I genuinely hope that my experiences and what I have learned can be a source of inspiration and guidance for you.

In the chapters ahead, I share stories about myself, revealing vulnerable moments and realizations contributing to how I was living and feeling as a military spouse. You don't have to be a military spouse to be able to relate to the struggle. I'm speaking to military spouses and women in today's society. It's important to know that many women think they are the only ones struggling, much like you may feel right now. This is why it's so important to share our stories. You'll read about my incredible clients, who found transformation through the steps we took together in searching for their answers. May their experiences highlight the endless possibilities that await you.

In Part I, I'll share my personal story of being a military spouse before and after my husband's retirement. We'll unravel the intricate challenges that make it difficult for women to take their turn and put their self-care and priorities first. We'll explore the Messy Web of complexities that contributes to this. As we transition to Part II, I'll introduce you to my C.A.L.M. method—a transformative approach I developed as a health and wellness coach. C.A.L.M. stands for Clarity, Awareness, Learning, and Mindset. We'll go into the details of each element: using Clarity as your compass to guide you to what you want, Awareness of what's slowing you down, Learning to listen to your body, and cultivating a Mindset of saying yes to yourself. Finally, in Part III, we'll wrap up with empowerment, summarizing the tools and giving you the encouragement to confidently take your turn.

My intention is for you to discover *your* answers and understand that you're not alone. I hope you feel empowered to initiate the changes you desire in your life, unraveling the internal struggles accompanying your unspoken desires. Those struggles are real. It's a narrative that resonates with the exhaustion of a busy life despite the blessings surrounding us. The ache is real, and introspection is needed to help you get to the other side of what you may be experiencing. You are absolutely worthy of it!

I want you to see the woman in the mirror, recognizing her beautiful essence and witnessing her strength and glow. This can be achieved by cultivating the love for the remarkable woman you are by forging a deeper connection with yourself. Imagine the future version of yourself living out your vision as a woman infused with purpose and passion for your life. As you prioritize giving to yourself first, you will understand that nurturing your well-being provides even more love and support for your family and those around you.

So let's confront the unknown together—and enter that uncomfortable space where we question who we want to be and where we're headed. **This journey is a testament to the liberating power of speaking our truths aloud, acknowledging vulnerabilities, claiming our worth, and recognizing the need for rest in a relentless world.** There's immense joy in witnessing women grant permission slips to care for themselves. It's always possible to change and pursue what you truly want. I'm here to support you in believing that you can do that.

May you discover strength in the beauty of confronting your story to become the person you truly want to be, and I encourage you to take all the time you need to do it. I'm thrilled to accompany you on this journey.

PART I

Chapter 1

It's Your Turn

It's a beautiful day inside the National Naval Aviation Museum in Pensacola, Florida. Warm summer sunshine filters through the windows. The display of the iconic Blue Angels is in formation overhead, suspended from the ceiling. Friends and family are gathering to put an exclamation point on my husband, John's, military career with a retirement ceremony.

A hush falls over the crowd as the clock strikes the top of the hour. The commanding officer, chaplain, and my husband step forward to make their formal entrance. Their presence commands respect and attention. I settle into my front-row seat with our son Kyle, daughter Kaitlyn, and our parents.

The bosun pipe whistles, followed by a crisp, loud voice announcing the official party's arrival. "Attention on deck!" The military members snap to attention and the crowd rises. As each official party member's name is announced to take the stage, the service member renders a crisp salute with a sharp snap of their arm, as if welcoming special guests aboard a Navy ship in port.

I can't help but marvel at the history surrounding us in the museum. There are many aircraft and historical pieces from previous generations, alongside photographs of the people who were part of that particular moment. Service members sacrifice so much. My thoughts go immediately to the families, especially the military spouses. They aren't in the pictures, but I know they quietly served right alongside their service member. I wonder if those spouses felt the same relief I'm feeling today when their time in the military came to a close.

John takes the stage and starts his speech, recalling our journey. The memories flash through my mind of the different places we lived, where our kids went to school, where Kyle first learned how to ride his bike, and the joy in Kaitlyn's laughter with her wonderful kindergarten teacher, Mrs. Russell. The guests are taken on a roller coaster of emotions, from laughter to tears. My heart swells as he shares his gratitude for working with some of the best people and caring for his patients as a Navy doctor.

John is fighting back tears as he shares the memorable stories of saying farewell to friends who became family, friends who were injured, and friends he lost.

I tell myself to hold in my tears and stay strong. If I lose it, he will lose it. We need this ceremony to grieve, let go of the things we have no control over, and celebrate the many things we are so grateful for.

As John concludes his speech, the kids and I are asked to come to the stage. The commanding officer reads a recognition to each of us for supporting our service member. The photographer is snapping pictures to mark the occasion. With certificates in hand, we return to our seats. Several traditional gifts are presented to my husband, recognizing him by the members in his command. A few minutes later, John walks off the stage, delivering flowers and kisses to Kaitlyn, our moms, and me. He then walks over to shake hands and shares hugs with Kyle and our dads.

While reading the beautiful poem, "Old Glory," four Navy service members stand in a line, each representing a rank John held during his time in the military. They deliberately pass a folded American flag from one set of hands to the next. I hold my breath as each service member handles the flag with reverence and care.

Finally, the flag reaches the end of the line to John. He walks over to me. Without knowing what would happen next, he bends down and gives me a sweet kiss. Then he hands me the folded flag and whispers, "I love you, and now, **it's your turn**."

With my voice quivering, I respond, "I love you too."

As he returns to his seat on the stage, my body is tingling with emotions. I look at the folded flag in my lap and have so many thoughts running through my head. *I am one of the lucky ones. John came home. He's still with me! We made it!!*

I can't keep it in any longer. The tears fall down my cheeks as the pressure of the life we have been living starts to release. My shoulders drop. My heart rate slows. I exhale. I have not felt this sensation of calmness in a long time.

For so many years, I kept my eye on the next move, the next job search, the next house, the next school for the kids . . . keeping all the balls up in the air . . . while holding my breath. Never letting one ball drop because it would mean I had failed as a military spouse, wife, and mom. The pressure of keeping up with everything in my life had been intense. My body knew it.

Many women do an unbelievable job executing many tasks, but we don't always put ourselves on the list as a priority. There are so many things we put ahead of caring for ourselves. I always had thoughts like, *When do I have time to take care of myself?* or *I'll take care of myself when . . . we get to the next duty station or when the kids get settled into the next school or when my husband returns from his work trip,* and on and on.

My excuses blurred with the demands of everyday life. I felt trapped because I had become defined by what I was *doing* rather than being true to who I wanted to *be*. I did everything a good military spouse should do (or at least the version of the "good military spouse" in my head). Still, I never felt like I was answering the call to take care of myself or have my own identity.

I always joked, "What will I be when I grow up?" but I never had an answer. I had what I like to call a "curvy" employment history, including being a registered respiratory therapist, "professional" volunteer, administrative assistant, financial analyst, and project coordinator. However, my career didn't feel like something I was advancing. It was always about adapting to the new surroundings and taking advantage of the best job or volunteer opportunity that worked for our family until the next move.

Along the way, there were ten moves with overseas assignments and deployments, multiple job changes, two fabulous and very flexible kids, and a supportive husband to help battle the stressful lifestyle. Although I found meaning in being a wife and mom, I couldn't help feeling like something was missing. While caring for everyone else, I had lost sight of who I was and what I wanted for myself, leaving me feeling lost and unfulfilled.

As I sat in the hour-long ceremony, I felt an immense weight lift, dissolving the heavy burden of worry and uncertainty that had plagued me for so long. It was like a clearing fog, allowing me to glimpse what lay ahead. For too long, I had underestimated the chaos that had become a part of our daily lives, zapping my joy and excitement for life. But unfortunately, my "fight or flight" button was stuck in the "on" position. I couldn't see it, but I was burnt out.

After the ceremony, relief washed over me. We were finally taking a step towards letting go of our unpredictable lifestyle. This filled me with a newfound sense of hope and optimism for what the future held, despite not knowing what exactly that was.

We drove over the three-mile bridge to a beach house we had rented for the week with our family. I couldn't help but think of the significance of crossing that bridge. It looked so different driving back from the ceremony than it had looked just a few hours before. It was as if my senses woke up. The water beneath us was so calm that it looked like glass, and it was an even deeper blue.

There were so many gifts that day; the best one for me was that time slowed down long enough for me to appreciate it. It was as if we were getting control back over our lives after a twenty-year roller coaster of uncertainty. Was that exhale at the ceremony making space for the goodness that would come in our next chapter?

The week after the ceremony, our new civilian life felt very different than the week before. We were still on an emotional high from having such an enjoyable beach week celebrating with friends and family. Time had slowed down.

As John and I were working on different projects around the house, I was in my home office doing some organizing. I cleared the papers on my desk and noticed a stack of brightly colored sticky notes. Thinking back to how good that exhale felt at the ceremony, I took a deep breath in, exhaled, and decided it was time. I savored John's words. *It IS my turn*, I thought.

On a bright, neon-yellow sticky note I wrote, "Today is the day I start taking care of ME first."

I posted it on my paper calendar to remind myself I have a choice each day. Even though our future was a little uncertain, this was a new birth for both of us, especially for me. The last twenty years were just a part of our story, *AND* there was still a more significant part to be written. I was no longer just the "dependent." I now had choices as a wife, mom, and career woman.

As soon as I realized that I *get to* choose who I want to be, I started to see the door of possibilities open. John and I decided to take a few months off to decompress. We took a Mediterranean cruise, just the two of us. I couldn't recall the last time we had taken a trip as a couple that didn't involve a move or a work conference. We started looking at ways to plant new seeds in different areas of our lives. I had to learn how to take time to get clear on what I wanted and release the pressure of having it all figured out in a set amount of time. I focused on re-establishing what was important to me in my relationships, career path, spiritual life, finances, energy level, and health. And resting was the first step!

After a summer of learning how to slow down, I discovered a job listing for a health educator. One of the requirements was to become a National Board Certified Health & Wellness Coach. I was curious about what that meant, so I did some research and could feel my excitement rise as I learned more. Health and wellness coaching was not just about improving numbers on the scale or metrics like blood work levels by eating better and moving more. There was more to it. It was about exploring a more profound sense of self-discovery and curiosity about an individual's beliefs, thoughts, and emotions.

It was a refreshing way to look at how every area of life can impact overall well-being. Bells started to go off in my head. This felt like my path, one that spoke to the deepest parts of my soul and filled me with an overwhelming sense of purpose and belonging.

My view of the military lifestyle had made me believe my own needs as a spouse weren't as big of a priority as the other demands in my life. I had this recording in my head playing over and over that I didn't have time to take care of myself. I bought into that belief for so many years. It showed up in how I cared for myself, nourished my body, handled my stress, and neglected my sleep habits.

Finally, I decided I was ready to invest in myself in a whole new way. I was worth it! I enrolled in a dual health and life coaching program to begin my new path as a coach. During the training, I realized it answered many things I struggled with. I found ways to reduce my stress, change my eating habits, add enjoyable movement, appreciate the present moment (especially time with family and friends), and do the things I really wanted to do to enjoy my life again. It wasn't an overnight transformation but a step-by-step learning journey to listen to my intuition and trust myself.

After completing my training, I focused on my new career as a health and wellness coach, and it became my mission to help women believe that they too can say YES to themselves and create the life they want.

I do this by helping women realize what it means to nourish themselves, handle stress better, and implement self-care practices that help them feel alive with purpose.

A big part of this involves changing our relationship with time so that we take care of our bodies and believe we are worth it. The world needs much more support and love right now, and the first step is for women to start taking better care of themselves. You are the most valuable asset in your life. Once you fill up your cup, goodness flows out to your families, friends, and the world around you, and positive things happen. It creates a ripple effect! *The world wants this for you!*

I don't believe you picked this book by accident. You may have lost a part of yourself along the way by being the "do it all" woman. Maybe you've been helping your partner in their career and, little by little, you feel like you're losing yourself in your marriage. Or that your only accomplishments are tied to your spouse's or kids' successes. Even with the many good things around you, you may feel empty.

This is your ultimate permission slip to take charge of your life and become the unstoppable, incredible woman you were always meant to be! I am here to inspire you with my personal journey, clients' success stories, and transformative teachings so you can break free from feeling stuck and embrace a life of abundance and fulfillment.

We are in this together. It's time for you to say YES to YOU, feel alive with purpose, and claim the life you truly deserve.

I'm so glad you are here.

Chapter 2

The Messy Web

A woman dressed in a casual floral shirt, khaki shorts, and flip-flops introduced herself as the PTO president and jumped right into the agenda.

She appeared to be organized but gave off the vibe of living on the edge in a "fly by the seat of her pants and just survive the day" kind of way. As she announced each project, she looked up and asked for a volunteer to take the lead. The list included many activities, like an upcoming book fair, the parent open house, the teacher appreciation luncheon, and fundraising events. Each time there would be a moment of awkward silence, then someone would eventually raise their hand.

Several moms in the room were familiar to me from meetings I had attended in other groups since arriving on the island of Guam as our new duty station. Some were from the military base church as religious education teachers for their kids' class, members of the spouse support group, coaches of their kid's soccer team, or the den mom for their son's Scout troop. What struck me the most was that each woman appeared to be doing a pretty good job balancing all the plates they had spinning despite the weary look in their eyes.

According to my watch, this meeting was going way over schedule. The president had transformed from a happy cheerleader to a woman pleading to get a giant load of projects off her shoulders. The other moms looked down to avoid eye contact, and an increasingly uncomfortable silence settled over the room. An overwhelming feeling of guilt convinced me that I wasn't doing enough and needed to do more. She announced the last event again, and it was as if I had no control over my body; it just happened. My hand raised all on its own.

This was when I began suffering from what I now call the *helium hand*. **The woman with the *helium hand* says "yes" to everyone else but herself.** She puts the needs of others before answering her own needs. She walks a tightrope between caring for her family and giving her time and talents to either a career or helping foster a better community.

It starts small, with one commitment and then another. Her responsibilities grow as others see her willingness to help and her ability to get things done. The curse of overachieving is the invitation to take more on. The accolades help fill the void of worthiness in her career or life. The thirst to use her talents is quenched. Before she knows it, boundaries are blurry or nonexistent, becoming a cycle that is hard to break.

It's difficult to see the physical, mental, and emotional cost until the signals of fatigue and exhaustion build in her body as she takes more on. Eventually, it leads to skipping meals and missing doctors' appointments to attend meetings, giving up workouts to volunteer in her child's classroom, and sacrificing date nights as couple time gets replaced with required social commitments. If she doesn't pay attention, this could lead to burnout and–even worse–adverse health issues. This was me.

Many women, not just military and service spouses, believe we must do everything. I understand the intense burden of feeling like we have to "do all and be all" for everyone. It's a weight we carry with us every day, from the moment we wake up until we finally collapse into bed at night. We've convinced ourselves that we must adopt the all-or-nothing approach to living our lives.

We have to stop believing this. It's not true, and the way out starts with detangling the Messy Web entrapping us.

The Messy Web

Women take on an incredible emotional load with raising a family, career demands, and keeping up with the needs of a household. The *helium hand* is part of the Messy Web I was trapped by, and I didn't even realize it.

There is a complex web of reasons why women take on so much and keep raising their hands. It runs deeper than we are willing to give credit to, with undercurrents of self-worth, identity, volunteerism, perfectionism, the guilt of disappointing someone, and so much more. The pressure to keep up with everything is reinforced by the messages we get from societal beliefs that we have to wear a cape and do it all. The stressors of a lifestyle like military life, having a spouse with an incredibly demanding career, or being the sole breadwinner for your family can feed into this cycle. We are in a time where the pressure is enormous to be a mom *and* CEO of the household *and* a contemporary woman with a successful and meaningful career.

The expectation to balance motherhood and career is not solely derived from societal beliefs but also cultural norms and personal beliefs shaped by observing the women in our lives. The pressure on women to prioritize their roles as caregivers and homemakers over their professional aspirations has been frustrating for generations. And for military and service spouses, this burden is amplified.

It's not just the household responsibilities they must handle but also the emotional strain of managing every aspect of family life, often alone. Service members are deployed or can have a high operational tempo where their daily schedules are filled with an extremely fast-paced volume of missions, exercises, and activities, keeping them away from their families and often facing increased stress and demands in their jobs. This constant weight of societal expectations and cultural messages can feel suffocating, leaving military spouses feeling overwhelmed and unsupported.

In this chapter, we will confront the many challenges that make prioritizing our well-being as women difficult. We will examine the web of intricate connections involving purpose, adaptability, sacrifices, meaning, life transitions, financial considerations, and self-worth. This intricate web affects us profoundly. But as we break down these complex parts and see how they connect, we gain the power to overcome the obstacles that stop us from being our best selves for our own sake and for those we care about. That's why we must go through this before we start to untangle our own webs. Let's examine this web, and then let's untangle it together in Part II.

You don't have to be a military spouse to be experiencing the web of messiness in your life. So many women are walking this tightrope, and I want you to know you are not alone. Chronic low-level stress, resulting from the challenge of this Messy Web and other unspoken causes, can lead to various physical and mental health problems. It's time we highlight why women need to care for themselves now more than ever.

Our unhealthy ways create havoc in our minds, bodies, relationships, workplaces, and communities. It's quietly seeping in and being passed on to our kids, partners, coworkers, and friends. By addressing the root causes of this, we can be the ones who recognize and decide it's time to break a cycle that is slowly taking away our joy and love for ourselves and others.

Let's dive deeper into the Messy Web of chaos.

Finding Purpose in a Life of Transitions

We were getting comfortable in our new home after a few months on the island of Guam. I volunteered as a parent helper in Kyle's homeroom and a few days a week at a military nonprofit. I also cooked dinners for young single sailors at our church. Despite this busy schedule, I really wanted to find a job. However, the opportunity to work in the medical field as a respiratory therapist was nonexistent for me because the base hospital had corpsmen covering the duties of respiratory therapists. Also, there were limited jobs at the local community hospital.

Nevertheless, I chose to channel my energy into something positive and meaningful. I eagerly welcomed the opportunity to connect with other military spouses. I longed for friendship and community to help battle the loneliness. I poured my heart and soul into helping build a sense of belonging in our small, tight-knit community. I felt a strong emotional tug on my heart and wanted to help other spouses do the same. It was a profoundly moving and fulfilling experience for me. The flexibility of being a volunteer was helpful, especially with young kids and a husband with an unpredictable schedule. The need was so great I felt I could not say no.

After a year on the island, I found myself not only volunteering in more groups but taking on leadership roles. Now, I was that woman leading the meetings and flying by the seat of her pants. I was organized enough to appear to have it all together but was doing backflips to meet all the demands and get other women to join in the madness.

The responsibilities grew, and most days, it felt like I was on a treadmill that I could not keep pace with. I started sacrificing my own needs–like skipping exercise time to attend evening meetings, staying up late to finish a project while the kids were in bed, and getting up before my alarm to prepare for the day. I had *no* time for me scheduled in my calendar. If I was fatigued, I was too busy to notice. I was in the weeds of living my everyday life, just planning (and surviving) to get to the next day. My heart was full temporarily, but I didn't know that I was stuck in a pattern and the burnout was coming.

I was honored to receive an award as the Navy's military spouse volunteer of the year before we left Guam. While I was proud of that award, I can't help but look back at it now as if I was rewarded for not taking care of myself. That was on me, but it wasn't all my fault. It was part of a web more significant than me. A vicious cycle of societal expectations and attitudes forced me to believe I had to self-sacrifice to get everything done.

When it was time for a move, I would pass the baton of responsibilities to another woman, thinking I'd finally get a break. But that break never happened. It was time to pack up, move to a new location, and start all over again.

The Power of Adaptability & Embracing Change

I didn't realize how much being a military spouse impacted my identity until my husband's retirement. My identity and the role I had had for twenty years changed in an hour-long ceremony. Looking back at my time as a military spouse, I was constantly the chameleon, adapting to my surroundings with each duty station. I was a master at doing what needed to get done. Military spouses are known for their resourcefulness and ability to handle challenges, and I was no exception. I always had a backup plan (or two) in case things didn't go as planned.

Every time we moved, we hit the ground running. Our family became experts at settling in fast. We knew the importance of quickly making our new living arrangement feel like home. We would unpack our belongings, hang the curtains on the windows and pictures on the walls, and find our church community. Then, John would get into his work routine. I would focus on getting Kyle and Kaitlyn settled in school and extracurricular activities to make new friends.

Then, the question would arise, "Where can I fit in?" I would start the job search, and it sometimes would take months before securing employment. To cope with the isolation and loneliness, I threw myself into volunteer work or took on jobs where I was underemployed. This term is frequently used within the military spouse community to describe being highly skilled or qualified but accepting a job that does not require one's full level of expertise.

Often, I would take whatever job fit best for our family at that particular time, with little regard for doing work that might compensate me for my experience or light up my soul. I found certain types of work fulfilling, particularly my volunteer work in our military community. However, other jobs didn't bring me the same sense of satisfaction. Growing up in a small rural community in Northwest Ohio, my parents and family taught me the importance of working hard, helping others, and giving from the heart. These values were ingrained in me from a young age and have stayed with me throughout my life.

So, even though I held jobs that didn't compensate or fulfill me completely, I remained inspired by my family's beliefs that emphasized the importance of doing the right thing, making the best of any situation, putting in my best effort, and never giving up. While these traits are admirable, they can be a double-edged sword, pushing you deeper into the web.

The Invisible Sacrifice of Supporting Your Spouse's Career

John and I grew up together. We dated in high school and continued our relationship through college. We married after I got my first full-time job as a respiratory therapist right out of college while he finished his undergraduate degree. Together, we decided that he would join the Navy to serve our country and help pay for his graduate education.

As John pursued his graduate school degree, we supported each other. We packed up and moved to Texas for his graduate program while I worked as a respiratory therapist at several hospitals in those four years. Throughout our journey, we worked to achieve our shared life goals and envisioned a future we could build together.

However, as time passed, military life began to take over our shared path. What started as our own individual dream paths slowly turned into one. As a result, I began losing sight of my aspirations and felt like my dreams for a career were no longer valid or important. Nevertheless, I kept plugging along.

Reading former First Lady Michelle Obama's book *Becoming*, I was struck by how this narrative often plays out in a couple's relationship. She writes how she put her career on hold and moved to Washington, D.C., with Barack Obama, to support his political career.[1] Laura Bush faced similar challenges as First Lady while George W. Bush served as president of the United States. In her memoir, *Spoken from the Heart*, she writes about her struggle to find her own identity and purpose during her husband's presidency.[2]

Both women's stories highlight the complex dynamics in a relationship where one partner's professional ambitions take center stage at the cost of sacrificing the other partner's career goals and aspirations. Nevertheless, these women sought opportunities to utilize their skills and significantly contribute to causes that aligned with their passions. Reading about these high-profile women struggling with their identities was illuminating. If it was true for them, how many other women have experienced the same?

Rediscovering Meaning in My Life

As much as I was ready to transition out of military life and plant roots somewhere, I felt comfort in knowing my role as a military spouse. It was a challenging lifestyle, but strangely enough, it was also predictable. In the whirlwind of military life, I unveiled the innate planner, connector, and encourager within me. I charted our moves with military precision.

Purging, decluttering, and resetting our lives during each transition became an art form for me. I created connections, not just for myself but for those around me. I thrived on bringing people together, whether it was fellow military spouses, neighbors, or friends. My mission was to foster a sense of community to strengthen the bonds that held us together. I enthusiastically dove into organizations and became a cheerleader for causes close to my heart. Rather than being overwhelmed, **the chaos became the canvas on which I painted my strengths.**

But to slow down and tell you who I was and my dreams? Those parts of me felt hidden. It was like stashing away those last few boxes in a closet after a move, promising to deal with them in a few weeks, only to have time slip away and find ourselves packing them up again for the next move. The uncertainty and constant change left me feeling lost and struggling to hold onto any sense of identity.

In our civilian life, I struggled to discover who I was and what I wanted. About a year after our transition out of military life, as I was building my coaching business, I attended a retreat that had a writing workshop. The assignment was to write our future biography. I was excited to write but froze, staring at a blank page, unable to describe even my current biography. I wanted to cry because I still could not write about myself and my dreams.

It started out easy: "I am a wife, a mom, and *was* a military spouse . . ." and then I rolled right into what my husband had done. I diminished everything I had done.

It became even more apparent when we had to share it with someone. After sharing the few sentences I had strung together with another attendee, she said, "You just told me everything your husband does; who are *you*?"

It was a punch in my gut. Suddenly, I could see why I couldn't write my biography. I was so focused on my husband's path and others that I couldn't even see mine. I was a cheerleader for everyone else in my life but me. As a result, I felt disconnected from myself and unsure of my own identity.

This may be your reality if you have taken a break from your career to raise a family or care for a loved one, like an elderly parent. You may be a woman who had a successful career and is now transitioning to the "What's next?" part of your life. Our identities are woven from the different roles we play and the things we do.

As a military spouse, it's easy to wrap our identity around being part of a community. "One team, one fight." There is a greater mission of service, and as military members and families, we have to be on board with that mission. Our loved one signed on the dotted line, and the military life and everything that comes with it became part of us whether we liked it or not.

Navigating the Bumpy Road of Transition to Civilian Life

When military couples transition from the end of their service to the civilian world, we leave a familiar community and navigate unknown waters. Each service member and their family's path is unique.

We had dreamed of the day for John to complete his time of service and establish some sort of normalcy for our family. There was a flurry of lists to take care of, and in true military fashion, we checked the boxes as we went. We were doing what needed to be done without really talking about what thoughts and emotions we were experiencing. In typical cadence, we were marching along with the mission. I wish someone had warned me of the emotional roller coaster of this transition. We experienced four struggles in our household at the same time.

First, John was navigating his new identity in the civilian workforce. It was the first time in twenty years he didn't have the daily reminder of his mission. Instead, he was finding his way to the next step in his career. He was seeking an organization that recognized the value of his military background and shared his principles of commitment, honor, trust, and service. It can be tricky for service members to find these shared values when transitioning to the civilian workforce.

Despite having valuable experience and leadership skills from his military career, securing a position that appreciated his expertise was challenging. It was difficult for civilian counterparts to understand the level and complexity of his leadership experience. He also had to transition with some aspects of civilian work, such as work attire, job application procedures, setting work-life boundaries, and building relationships.

Second, I struggled to figure out who I was as a woman, shifting roles as a mom and military spouse. As I watched our two young adults take the next step in their journey, a deep sense of grief and gratitude washed over me. I couldn't help but grieve the loss of the time that had gone by so quickly. Kyle and Kaitlyn were no longer the little ones who looked to me for help. I regretted taking things for granted when they were younger, such as the simple moments like reading a book to them before bed, packing their lunches for school, and feeling guilty for not baking cookies for them more often. Are there ever enough cookies?

As mothers, we are programmed to provide care and support for our children. But as they grow older, their needs change, and we have to learn to let go. We shift into a different role as an observer and mentor in their life, where they get to make decisions and mistakes and celebrate their wins. I am so proud of Kyle and Kaitlyn. They have blossomed into unique individuals, and I'm excited about who they are and their impact on the world.

As a military spouse, I constantly approached each job and even volunteered as if it were my own business, taking ownership and striving to make it a success. The entrepreneurial spirit within me craved the ability to make my own decisions, set my schedule, and align my choices with my values. I had decided to quit my job at this time. I didn't know for sure what I was going to do. But I began dreaming about owning my work and being my own boss.

Third, retirement from the military affects not only the service member and the military spouse but also the kids. Military kids are some of the most resilient humans on the planet despite the many challenges of being in a military family. I stand in awe of Kyle, Kaitlyn, and every military child as they navigate numerous moves, new schools, social connections for friendships, switching homes, and frequent separations from their service members.

It's not always easy. Finding consistent healthcare or education support can be difficult if the child has additional needs. If a service member has experienced trauma, especially the invisible scars of war, this can be something the spouse and kids take on without even realizing it. One of the most silent challenges for military families, especially military spouses and children, is the lack of control in their lives. As a parent, military spouses take on the invisible emotional needs to ensure our kids stay healthy socially, mentally, and emotionally.

Retirement from military service alleviates some of this; however, settling in one spot after so many moves can cause the family to question, "Where is home?" Reintegration as a family unit is often discussed after deployment, and reentering civilian life is no different. The family learns to navigate many things, especially the one foreign thing: stability.

Finally, we were navigating our relationship as a couple. Retirement brought a sense of liberation from the strictures of military life and uncertainty about what would be ahead. We had more time to spend with each other, learned to balance household duties, and grew friendships in our community. There were some bumpy points, but it was a time of massive growth for both of us, individually and as a couple.

An essential piece in our evolution as a couple was ensuring we kept communicating with each other with a compassionate heart and understanding. It takes patience to slow down, learn to listen, and share your needs. We kept our attitudes in check and frequently had to remind each other that we were on the same team. Our love and respect for each other grew. Our conversations over time turned into dream dates. We were dreaming of what was possible for the future when we learned to focus on what we could control and calm the chaos within us.

Our relationship is still evolving even years after transitioning out of military life. We've found peace in learning to live one day at a time, being present in the moment, and not always being focused on the next thing.

I understand how times of change can be scary. It can take an enormous emotional toll on you as a woman. I realized that to end the cycle of chaos and figure out what I wanted for myself, I needed to prioritize my needs, let go of certain things, and establish habits that would promote my overall well-being. John and I both had to do this. Forming a new identity requires time to shed unrealistic expectations, beliefs we developed from our experiences, and unhealthy habits. Clearing the clutter in our lives made room for self-growth and many more opportunities.

After reflecting on my passions, interests, and goals, I realized I needed to reconnect with my path. So, I began to work on my dreams again, with the support of John, who understood the importance of pursuing our individual goals while still working towards a shared vision. As a result, we have created a fulfilling life together by finding a balance between our shared goals and personal aspirations. We learned to respect and celebrate each other as individuals for the unique gifts we brought to our relationship. Two paths are walking beside one another and cheering each other on again.

If you are wondering how to begin building your vision, keep reading. We'll discuss creating vision for your path to well-being in chapter 4, "Clarity is Your Compass."

The Financial Ripple

Families in our country struggle to make ends meet with rising living costs, stagnant wages, and debt. This financial strain causes even more stress, anxiety, and uncertainty when constantly worried about affordable housing, food, childcare, and future education costs. When both partners are employed, it can reduce the burden of financial responsibility and give each individual a feeling of empowerment by having a career. In today's economic climate, it can be challenging for households with only one source of income to provide their families with even their basic needs.

Employment has always been a challenging and stressful area for military spouses. Not having a steady career as a military spouse comes as a sacrifice to the entire family. The gaps in unemployment result in the loss of family income. The loss of income means more financial strain. The strain on finances means even more significant stress on a couple and family's relationships. The pressure on a couple's relationship and finances puts even more weight on an already stressful circus of moving logistics, extra expenses, deadlines, and the uncertainty of military life. The financial influence weaves through every complicated part of this messy web, like the moves, transition, employment, and even permission to invest in yourself.

As a veteran military spouse, I have a curvy employment history in different industries, with unemployment gaps between our many moves. Preparing to face the laborious job search and application process with every relocation was an emotional struggle. I reinvented myself at least a dozen times. However, I know I'm not alone after reading *The 2021 Blue Star Families Military Family Lifestyle Survey,* which showed that 47 percent of active-duty spouses were concerned about spouse employment, and 63 percent of active-duty spouses reported being underemployed.[3] It's an exhausting dance many military spouses have become accustomed to.

Frequent moves or unemployment gaps are hard to address in a resume without hinting you are a military spouse. I feared employers wouldn't even consider me if they knew I might only be at the company for just a few years before leaving for the next duty station. Being asked, "What does your spouse do?" in a job interview became a tricky question to navigate. While there is great pride in sharing your spouse's service and your family's experiences, many spouses are afraid to share the real story for fear of not getting a job.

Some military spouses are sacrificing career advancement, retirement savings, and other benefits otherwise provided with the stability of staying at a particular company. Even if spouses find a fantastic career opportunity, the time comes when the moving truck pulls up, and they are left to restart their lives all over again. It becomes a regular practice of restarting their professional life every two to three years.

Employment issues may make it difficult for military families to live together. It's not uncommon for a military service member to live as a "geographical bachelor," where the family chooses to stay at their current location while their service member lives in a different place for several years. Although this can assist families in avoiding unexpected moving expenses and provides stability for their children's education and spouse's employment, it creates other challenges for their families.

This includes child caretaking responsibilities falling to one spouse, added travel costs, increased housing expenses, and missed holidays and birthdays. Working a family schedule as a single parent for an extended time is daunting. The service member can feel the distance and loneliness. This impact on a service member's, spouse's, and family's health cannot be overlooked.

As you can see, there are many layers to this complicated issue of military spouse employment. While passionate and mission-based organizations advocate changes, much work remains. I'm grateful for the dedicated work and leadership of women like Sue Hoppin, founder and president of the National Military Spouse Network. Sue and the National Military Spouse Network team published the *2021 NMSM White Paper, Roadmap to Employment Stability for Military Spouses.*

The paper emphasizes recommendations for establishing financial security during a military family's service and points out that of the nearly one million military spouses, over one-quarter are actively seeking employment. This results in an unemployment rate of roughly 25 percent for military spouses, seven times higher than the national average.[4]

In the 2023 *NMSN White Paper, Solving the Military Spouse Puzzle*, 40 percent of military families have considered leaving active-duty service because of challenges associated with military spouse employment.[5] This ripple reaches far and wide because it negatively impacts retention rates to keep quality people in our military. This isn't just a military spouse issue. This is an issue that affects military retention rates and, ultimately, the security of our nation.

Several US administrations have prioritized promoting employment opportunities for military spouses, resulting in the launch of various initiatives aimed at supporting military families in this area.[6] The COVID-19 pandemic has also helped to begin to transform the employment landscape for military spouses, opening up new avenues to access job opportunities through remote work. Companies across various industries continue to forge partnerships to harness the valuable skills and qualities that military spouses bring to the table, now leveraging the power of virtual employment to make this a reality.

While much progress has been made, there is still a need for continued support and resources to address the unique challenges military spouses face in finding and maintaining employment.

You Are Worthy

Military spouses' employment struggles are more than a passing worry; they can strike at the core of one's well-being, especially worthiness.

It's a constant battle, leaving you questioning your purpose and meaning in life, particularly when you haven't been able to pursue a career with meaningful work. The feelings of self-worth, lack of confidence, guilt, and shame can swirl around, causing stress and even more chaos in your body. Your body (and mind) keep score. Exhaustion can set in, leaving you feeling drained and alone. The voices of military spouses sharing these struggles are evident through social media posts, virtual groups, and conversations, demonstrating the urgency of addressing well-being issues and supporting this valuable community.

Maybe you decided to step away from your career because you had to take the lead at home, you chose to be a stay-at-home mom, or you had to take care of an ailing parent. No matter the reason, there is a part of you that may not have allowed you to develop and grow as a woman in the professional area of your life. When society places so much value on what we accomplish and earn, especially in a career, we don't feel our part has been valuable if we aren't receiving a paycheck. This can chip away at the value you see in yourself, and others see in you. Whether or not we want to admit it, finances and worthiness are deeply related.

After John's military retirement, I was overwhelmed by years of grief stemming from my inability to grow professionally. The absence of my personal purpose and fulfillment left a void. I felt undervalued because I couldn't contribute significantly to our family's finances for so long.

John never made me feel unworthy, and he frequently expressed gratitude for the invaluable things I did for our family. However, my internal struggle fueled my feelings of unworthiness. For years, I coped by filling up my days with volunteer activities to prove my worth.

While writing this book, I read Glennon Doyle's book, *Untamed*, and jumped out of my cozy spot under the bed covers when I read these sentences.

"My worth is tied not to my productivity but to my existence. I am worthy of rest. Changing my root belief about worthiness has changed my life."[7]

YES! I felt validated. **For so much of my life, I had sacrificed my worth for everyone else to be comfortable but me.**

Sometimes, it's easy to feel dismissed as "just the dependent" or "a woman." This became apparent to me one day as I checked out at our local car dealership for car repairs. When I heard they offered military discounts, I proudly showed my dependent military ID card at checkout.

The gentleman looked at the card and replied, "I'm sorry, we only give discounts to the service member. You're just the spouse."

My face grew hot. I could feel my feelings inside boil like hot water in a teapot ready to whistle.

"*Just* the spouse!?" I said.

His eyes grew wide as he realized what he'd said. But it was too late.

I was working so hard as a military spouse and wasn't allowing myself to take the time to care for myself, making me feel even more resentful. And his words—*"just* the military spouse"—reinforced the value I was feeling for myself.

That day, I made a pivotal decision: I would no longer allow myself to be undervalued. I needed to value myself first. Then, it was time to start working on claiming my worth and helping women like you claim yours.

Who in your life is making you feel undervalued? Is it you or someone else? The stories we tell ourselves or believe based on what others say can cause us to fall into the trap of undervaluing ourselves. In chapter 5, "Awareness of What's Slowing You Down," we'll create awareness about those beliefs and how they slow us down as women. You're a woman of great value to your family and community. Now more than ever is the time to value yourself by caring for yourself and your needs.

The Invisible Load That Breaks Your Body

In 2010, we took orders to move to Annapolis, Maryland. We were excited to make the journey back stateside. With our extended family in Ohio and more employment opportunities, this would make things easier. Or so I thought. With growing kids and the pressure of future education expenses, I wanted to find full-time work to contribute to our family income.

I visited the Navy Fleet and Family Service Center to work with an employment representative to help me update my resume, which included adding my volunteer skills. It took multiple visits and several months, but eventually I landed a job as an administrative assistant at the United States Naval Academy. Taking the job and working for the federal government was a way to get my foot in the door to access better opportunities. Finally, I was ready to use my experience and talents and be compensated for what I could do.

Life took on a faster pace than ever before.

My days began with drinking several cups of coffee in the morning and would end with a few glasses of wine in the evening. I spent most days eating lunch while working at my desk. The pace ramped up even more after work, racing to the bus stop or after-school activities with dinner on the run or later that evening.

As time passed, I noticed how tired I was, but I always chalked it up to how busy we were as a family. So I would continue to press on each day. I did what needed to get done with little to no time scheduled to take care of myself. But then I started experiencing a sensation like I had marbles in my throat, irregular periods, heart palpitations, and trouble sleeping.

Throughout this time, I occasionally caught up with friends from college or other military spouses on the phone, and we would share what we had going on in our lives. Eventually, our conversations would end up mentioning our various bodily symptoms. We would laugh and jokingly say, "Forty is coming."

But I didn't want to buy into that story that forty was when our bodies started to break down. *Why is my body failing me?* Little did I realize that I was failing my body. I never questioned if my symptoms were related to one another, and I certainly didn't connect them to what was going on in my life. My body was begging me for attention. But I just kept pushing.

A few months later at my annual physical, my doctor came into the exam room with a warm smile and greeted me with urgency, like her hair was on fire. It was clear her time was precious. I realized I had to explain my health issues rapidly. As she did my physical exam, I barreled through my list of symptoms.

While wrapping up, as she took off her gloves, she asked me, "How is your stress level?"

Without hesitating, I said, "I'm good! My husband is home from deployment; it's slowed down some at work, the kids have adjusted to their new schools, and we're not moving this year, so yeah, it's all good!"

I didn't see any connection to how my symptoms had anything to do with my stress level. She referred me to other physicians specializing in gastroenterology and gynecology. I went to more appointments, followed by more tests and prescribed medications.

But it was no good—my symptoms never seemed to get better.

As a health and wellness coach, I can now see how my symptoms and fatigue were connected to the chaos. I also now realize that I was in perimenopause and didn't understand how stress might be aggravating my symptoms even more. Not one provider talked to me about perimenopause or how stress can exacerbate it.

I started writing this book during the COVID-19 pandemic before statistics were available to capture the real impact of how stressful lifestyles affect women and service spouses. Unfortunately, few health statistics provide information on the stress of service spouses. However, many health institutions recognize that women develop a higher rate of health issues due to exposure to chronic stress over long periods. These health problems include but are not limited to depression, anxiety, heart problems, headaches, obesity, gastrointestinal issues, autoimmunity issues, pregnancy complications, and menstrual issues.

Even Deloitte's *Women at Work 2022*, A Global Outlook study, spotlighted some of the pandemic's impact on women and their workload growth:

> Through the pandemic, women have taken on more responsibilities at home and work while not receiving adequate support from their employers. Nearly 80% of surveyed women indicate that their workload at work has increased due to the pandemic. At the same time, 66% of women report having the greatest responsibilities for home tasks, and more than half of those with children say they handle most childcare duties. The mounting responsibilities are taking a toll on their physical health, mental well-being, and career ambitions.[8]

Let's be honest: women have been grappling with symptoms of fatigue well before the pandemic, and these challenges have only intensified after the global health crisis. Bureau of Labor Statistics data from 2021 reveals that women spend approximately 3.5 hours more per week on housework than men, excluding errands, grocery shopping, and childcare.[9]

As women shoulder a more significant burden of traditional household chores, they also engage in numerous other tasks that often go unrecognized and unaccounted for. These tasks often involve deeper emotional and invisible labor. Allison Daminger's research, published in the *American Sociological Review*, comprehensively breaks down the mental load or cognitive labor into four components: anticipation, identification, decision-making, and monitoring. We can't fully comprehend the complexities of each task until we outline each in detail and acknowledge the steps involved.[10]

Consider the multitude of steps involved in tasks such as planning family travel, researching childcare options, managing appointments and repairs, handling financial expenses, worrying about a child's academic struggles, navigating relationships with extended family, attending to the needs of aging parents, and countless other responsibilities. Often, these tasks are taken for granted.

The cumulative impact of shouldering such an invisible load can profoundly affect our health and well-being. It is time to acknowledge, address, and support women's emotional and mental aspects of household labor. The stress buckets were already pretty full for so many people before 2020 and, with the COVID-19 pandemic, those stress buckets were overfilled and tipped.

The long-term effects may not show up in actual statistics and studies for quite awhile, but I'm pretty confident if you ask most women, the stress of being in a life where they just can't keep up affects nearly everything. It influences every part of our well-being: mental, emotional, physical, spiritual, physical environment, finances, relationships, and career.

Resentment Is Your Warning Light

Resentment acts as a subtle but significant clue, signaling the need to slow down and pay attention. In my own journey, the physical symptoms like marbles in my throat, heart palpitations, and trouble sleeping were the more obvious indicators that led me to seek medical help. However, I didn't recognize the quiet undercurrent of resentment, a simmering emotion beneath the surface. Resentment doesn't always manifest as boiling rage; it can quietly brew, building up over time. You may not realize it until you take a step back and reflect. **Looking back, I realized I harbored a quiet resentment, feeling unhappy about investing so much effort without adequate returns or exhausting myself while others seemed to thrive at my expense.**

The World Health Organization ties this exhaustion to burnout in the workplace:

> "Burnout is a syndrome that results from feelings of energy depletion or exhaustion, increased mental distance from one's job, or feelings of negativism or cynicism related to one's job and reduced professional efficacy."[11]

While I can appreciate the emphasis on the workplace, what if we looked at this from the perspective of our lives? Replacing the words "job" with "life" and "professional" with "personal?" Burnout is a syndrome that results from feelings of energy depletion or exhaustion, increased mental distance from one's life, or feelings of negativism or cynicism related to one's life and reduced personal efficacy.

It sounded exactly where I was. I'm guessing you may feel it too.

Through the many conversations I've had with women, the topics of stress, fatigue, exhaustion, and burnout often arise. One of the common feelings that surface is resentment. It's hard not to feel resentment when you are not taking the time for yourself or your needs. Likewise, resentment can show up when we feel unappreciated, disrespected, or unsupported.

Brené Brown has a powerful reference to this in her book, *Atlas of the Heart*: "Resentment is the feeling of frustration, judgment, anger, better than, and/or hidden envy related to perceived unfairness or injustice. It's an emotion that we often experience when we fail to set boundaries or ask for what we need or when expectations let us down because they are based on things we can't control, like what other people think, what they feel, or how they're going to react."[12]

Resentment can lead to bitterness and negative thought patterns that can harm our mental health and relationships. Resentment is a topic that comes up frequently in group coaching calls. Admitting resentment can help us know we have important work to do on and for ourselves. By creating this awareness, we can get curious about the cause of our resentment. This can help us experience a healing process that fosters personal growth, enhances our relationships, and ultimately transforms our lives.

To me, resentment is like the temperature gauge on a car. Maintaining a healthy and happy state is crucial to keeping it in check. When resentment shows up, it serves as your warning light that you and your body require some attention. Giving your body the self-care you need, like engaging in enjoyable activities, getting adequate sleep, eating nourishing foods, spending time with friends, and enjoying outside time, are healthy ways to help that temperature level decrease. This can involve setting time, energy, expectations, and thought boundaries.

When setting impossibly high standards for ourselves, we constantly battle feelings of guilt and inadequacy. Saying no can be difficult, but we can ask for help and delegate things to others to prioritize our well-being. It's okay to admit that we can't do everything and do it perfectly. We need support from those around us. We need to change our standards of what we expect from others, but more importantly, our expectations of ourselves.

When we do this for ourselves, we teach others it's okay to do the same. Let's release the grip of the all-or-nothing mentality and embrace a balanced approach to life. It's time to give ourselves permission to step back when necessary and prioritize what truly matters. After all, we're only human and deserve to navigate life with grace and compassion.

So, let's not waste a precious moment. With this newfound insight, we will forge a path forward, liberating ourselves from the entanglements that impede our well-being—aligning with our unique needs and desires. Just as I embraced the American flag at my husband's retirement ceremony and granted myself permission to take my turn, it is now your time to step forward and claim your turn too!

Chapter 2 Key Takeaways

- The Messy Web is a tangled web of complexities of purpose, adaptability, sacrifices, meaning, transitions, finances, and worthiness that make prioritizing ourselves challenging.

- It's important to unravel this intricate web and understand how the various parts can hinder our well-being.

- Women often shoulder a significant burden of tasks and responsibilities that go unrecognized, adding to stress and impacting their well-being.

- Resentment is the warning light telling us it's time to care for ourselves.

PART II

Chapter 3

Time to Calm the Chaos

As the train rolled steadily along the tracks, I gazed out the window, admiring the picturesque scenery passing by. The sun's warm rays illuminated the mountainous landscape, filling me with a sense of calm. Everything seemed clear and predictable, the path ahead promising and familiar.

But suddenly, the train plunged into a tunnel. The train car was engulfed in darkness, creating an eerie black veil around me, obscuring my surroundings. A wave of uncertainty washed over me, and the familiar comfort I had felt only moments ago evaporated into thin air. Fear and worry crept into my mind, whispering doubts about what awaited on the other side.

But in the midst of the darkness and my uneasiness, a gentle inner voice broke through the noise. It whispered, "Breathe. Trust." It was a reminder to tap into my inner strength. As I took a deep breath, the voice encouraged me to relinquish the need for control and surrender to the journey, even when the destination seemed uncertain.

A profound sense of peace washed over me. And just as suddenly as the darkness had descended, the train emerged from the tunnel, greeted by a breathtaking landscape of mountains and waterfalls bathed in the warm glow of sunlight. It was a visual reminder of the beauty that lies beyond our worries and fears, the rewards waiting for us when we choose to trust and let go.

Marie, one of my clients, had her own worry train when she faced her family's relocation to Tampa from Atlanta for her husband's job as an airline pilot.

"What will I do when I move? All my friends are here. I won't know anyone there. What if I don't make any friends? What if I hate it? What if I'm all alone? What about my new real estate business I just started?"

These questions consumed her mind, and I could see the overwhelm set in. I empathized deeply with her, sensing the weight of her fear, grief, and yearning for a sense of community. This connection was particularly emotional, considering the numerous relocations I had experienced as a military spouse. I understood her worries.

During our coaching call, we explored Marie's fears and the possibilities on the other side. I acknowledged her feelings and discomfort. I also wondered if she would be open to looking at her situation differently.

So I asked her, "What if it all works out? What if you make even more great friends? What if you love it there? What if your business grows and explodes with new opportunities?"

At first, Marie struggled to see beyond the darkness of the tunnel. She was trapped in her worries, unable to envision a positive outcome. But working together, her perspective began to shift. I challenged her to stop creating chaos in her mind and instead prepare herself for something even more glorious.

Over several months, Marie courageously embraced the lessons she had learned about herself and the empowering C.A.L.M. method with strategies we explored during our coaching sessions. With newfound determination, she released the grip of her fears and embraced the potential of a brighter future.

She explored new experiences by joining a business networking group in her new community. Marie savored the sweetness of creating deeper connections with other business owners who became friends. She developed habits of taking care of her needs. By discovering Marie's nonnegotiables, she showed up as a confident version of herself. And her newfound real estate business thrived because of her unwavering belief in herself and her abilities.

Life is full of uncertainties. There will always be twists, turns, and unexpected detours. In those moments when the train is hurtling through a dark tunnel, fear may grip our hearts, and doubts may cloud our minds. But it is in those very moments that we have a choice. We can choose to confront our fears, trust in the process, and let go of the need for control. We can calm the chaos within us.

This is the path I have been gifted as a health and wellness coach, guiding women like Marie through their intricate pathways of uncertainty and chaos to a calm, balanced, peaceful life. I crafted the C.A.L.M. method—Clarity, Awareness, Learning, and Mindset—as a way to liberate myself and my clients from the spin of daily living to recalibrate, rediscover our inner compass, and live each day on our terms. This method empowers you to embrace a new way of nourishing yourself by giving yourself the resounding "yes" you deserve.

Throughout this journey, we will explore the steps of my foundational coaching approach. Whether you take this journey within a supportive community, guided by a coach, or independently, these steps universally apply to any goal you set for yourself. I have distilled these steps from my personal experiences and from guiding hundreds of clients, uncovering the four stages that lead to taking inspired action. Choosing "yes" for yourself begins a life that aligns with your desires. As we explore the upcoming chapters, you'll learn how to get your transformation through the lens of my C.A.L.M. method. Here's how it breaks down.

CLARITY

As we dive into clarity in chapter 4, "Clarity is Your Compass," we uncover the gift of pausing to cultivate space in our lives for moments of quiet, rest, and fully embracing the present moment. By living in the art of being you, you begin to take action as the person you want to show up in your life.

This is an opportunity to connect to who you are, discover your "why," and the significance of your core values and how to use them to find your true inner strengths. You'll learn the connections between the different aspects of your life and how they impact one another. These foundational elements lay the groundwork for creating a vision that truly resonates with your soul.

Through engaging and insightful reflections, you'll gain a newfound clarity that empowers you to navigate the twists and turns of your growth journey. It's a vital step that guides you in discovering where you want to go and creating a map to reach your desired destination.

AWARENESS

The second step in chapter 5, "Awareness of What's Slowing You Down," involves becoming aware of the self-limiting beliefs holding you back. What stops you from being who you are or getting what you want? As we journey into understanding, I will unravel the most common obstacles hindering women or preventing them from embracing their full potential. These beliefs often stem from our past experiences or negative thought patterns. By identifying them, you can begin to challenge and change them. This is where self-awareness becomes a powerful tool.

During this step, your focus will shift toward fostering a sense of curiosity to recognize the behaviors and beliefs that make you feel stuck or realize what has been slowing you down.

But that's not all–I'm extending you an invitation to recognize the obstacles without criticism and, with self-compassion, discover the value in these challenges as essential stepping stones in your personal growth. It's about acknowledging that these limiting beliefs are not truths but stories you've told yourself or others convinced you of. You have the power to reframe these stories into more empowering thoughts.

As we progress through this step, you'll build an awareness that shines a light on these obstacles and then propels you forward with the belief shift you can adopt to lead you toward meaningful change. Becoming aware of what is slowing you down is essential to this process. Creating a new belief is liberating and powerful for your inner growth and progress for change.

LEARNING

As we step into the third phase of the C.A.L.M. method in chapter 6, "Learning to Listen to Your Body," you'll discover the craft of listening to your body—a skill often underestimated in the chaos of modern life. You'll learn the value and ways to listen to your body and begin to understand and honor your body's actual needs.

We'll dive deep into the impact of stress on our lives and the necessity of understanding how it affects every facet of our well-being. We'll consider the importance of managing chronic low-level stress by sharing different ways to satisfy your need for rest. We'll look at how decluttering your environment can help clear your mind, and how strong social connections determines your longevity. You'll discover the power and the significance of meal prepping and balanced nutrition on your energy level.

We'll explore what works best for how you get to move your body and put together the right puzzle pieces you need for the rejuvenating effects of quality sleep. Through collaboration, we'll construct a straightforward blueprint that sets the tone with intention and empowers you to prioritize what resonates with you while celebrating every step.

Learning to listen to your body means harnessing your intuition and wisdom to discover your inner balance, allowing you to recognize and honor your body's signals for a more nourished life.

MINDSET

In the final step of the C.A.L.M. method, chapter 7, "Mindset of Saying "Yes" to Yourself," we will explore the fundamental role of mindset in shaping our lives and experiences. Learning how to turn your thoughts into powerful actions, reframing your limiting beliefs, claiming your worth, and cultivating compassion and self-love will be at the core of this chapter. You'll understand the importance of celebrating progress and surrounding yourself with a supportive community. By embracing possibilities and abundance through gratitude, this part of the C.A.L.M. method empowers women to take action and wholeheartedly say "yes" to themselves, paving the way for a more fulfilling life.

As we venture into this life-changing path together, placing your needs at the forefront might feel intimidating, particularly if you fear it will disrupt your world. But this can be accomplished without the weight of overwhelm or guilt. Crafting a tailored plan that encompasses every facet of your life is achievable. You can shatter the limiting beliefs that have confined you to an unsustainable routine, and it's possible to live a purposeful life with simplicity as your guide.

Just as Marie and many others before you have done, you possess the power to emerge from the shadows and bask in the brilliance that lies ahead, knowing the time for you is now. Remember, even within the darkest tunnels, there's always a glimmer of light beckoning you forward.

The time has come to unleash your inner radiance, allowing it to illuminate the path to the life you are meant to live. With the C.A.L.M. method as your guide, you'll tackle challenges and celebrate triumphs, fully aware that you can step into your brilliance and shine brightly.

It's time to reclaim your essence and forge a stronger relationship with the most vital person in your life—YOU.

Chapter 3 Key Takeaways

- The C.A.L.M. method—Clarity, Awareness, Learning, and Mindset—empowers you to embrace a new way of nourishing yourself by giving yourself the resounding "yes" you deserve.

- It's possible to live a purposeful life with simplicity as your guide.

Chapter 4

Clarity Is Your Compass

*Our intuition is like a muscle; we must practice
listening to it and trusting its wisdom.*
—Lisa Prosen

One of my favorite childhood memories is of my grandparents sitting on their front porch in their rockers. If we were to stop over for a visit, most evenings we would find them in their chairs on the front porch, waving to friends and neighbors as the local traffic and world went by. Their life wasn't always this quiet. They raised ten kids together. I can't imagine the silence that hit their house when the last kid launched into the world.

I hadn't truly experienced the beauty of slowing down and embracing silence until the unexpected arrival of the COVID-19 pandemic. I understand that this time was incredibly chaotic and challenging for so many. In my case, the situation took on a unique aspect due to my family's particular stage of life.

As the world grappled with the pandemic's upheaval, my coaching business was already accustomed to remote video calls before Zoom became a household name. John navigated the transition of his teaching and medical responsibilities to a temporary virtual platform. Meanwhile, Kyle returned home to complete his final college semester, and Kaitlyn finished her senior year of high school. They did this from the confines of their bedrooms–a scenario familiar to countless students.

Despite the chaos in our world, we found a rhythm to our day. Our mornings started with breakfast together, and then we went to our designated spaces to work. We would break to have lunch and then return to our rooms for the afternoon. John and I would end our workday with a late afternoon walk in our neighborhood. As our evening time was cleared from canceled activities, I took full advantage of tackling some projects I had procrastinated on, like cleaning out closets, organizing the garage, clearing email inboxes, organizing pictures, and other decluttering. Even though there was some resistance, my family joined in to help.

It felt good to slow down. Being forced to stay in one spot was what I needed to catch up with myself and life.

During this time, John and I started reevaluating what was important in our lives. As we deliberately carved out moments in our day, sharing a cup of coffee while sitting on the patio or enjoying an evening walk at the beach, our conversations organically morphed into a vivid vision of what lay ahead. This vision included everything from finding a new home, expanding our professional careers, and planning the adventures to those dream destinations we'd jotted down on our bucket list. I felt relieved whenever the idea of moving to a smaller, more manageable home came to mind. I could feel the lightness of a simple life, which was liberating and motivating.

After days of spirited back-and-forth conversations about whether to take the plunge, we reached a turning point. In a move fueled by equal parts courage and trust in our instincts, we reached out to our close friend, Cindy, who also happened to be a real estate agent. Within a few hours of our conversation, our home went on the market to sell. We chose to remain in the local area and opted for another neighborhood as part of our effort to downsize and simplify. Even during a global pandemic, we were determined to make this change, and at times, I couldn't help but marvel at the audacity of our decision.

But we weren't the only ones looking to make life changes. We noticed many people from colder parts of the country interested in moving to the Florida panhandle. They wanted to exchange staying inside during gloomy days for enjoying the sunny weather, and they preferred taking care of their lawns all year round instead of shoveling snow. So it wasn't long before we had an offer on our house.

With the sale of our house in early summer, our lives picked up pace again. John decided to do a one-year specialty training program in Virginia, over seven hundred miles away. He had been talking about doing this training for twenty years. I was overjoyed he was finally embracing his dream and passion for learning. Despite the challenges of spending a year apart, we knew we could navigate this situation with little trouble from the experiences and skills we'd gained during our twenty-year military life. Transitioning to civilian life, we found ourselves better equipped to handle our logistical separations, given the strength of our bond and the resilience we had developed in our relationship as a couple.

After we moved most of our household items into temporary storage, John took off to start his training. I helped Kaitlyn move to South Florida, where she eagerly stepped into her first year of college, excited for the start of her grand new adventure. While coordinating logistics between the sale of our house and moving to our new home, Kyle and I ended up in a furnished rental for a few months.

Upon arrival, I entered this charming, beautiful cottage, which instantly felt like an oasis. The room was colored with a soft palette of blue, beige, and white, making it feel like you were stepping into a quiet, little beach retreat. I observed the side door that opened into an enclosed patio while peering through the windows, allowing the warm sunlight to pour in. As I made my way onto the screened-in porch surrounded by lush green bushes and trees, there was a row of rocking chairs overlooking the waters of Pensacola Bay—another invitation to slow down. Even though most Florida days were brutally hot, I was drawn to those chairs each day during our stay. No phone, no obligations, just me, the rocking chair, and my thoughts. Silence and stillness became something I craved.

You can learn much about yourself and the world by slowing down and practicing being still. It can be a powerful gateway to valuable lessons about your true self and deepest desires. You uncover hidden truths, discover new perspectives, and immerse yourself in the beauty of being present and living in the moment. It's an invitation to reconnect to your mind and body.

Even though I quit my job in 2018 to discover what my heart wanted, I didn't have to give up my career this time. And you don't either to get clarity in your life. I learned the tools to recognize and develop an awareness of when I was being pulled back into the Messy Web and then took the time to find the clarity I needed. It took curiosity, no judgment, and just a few minutes to be still. This could look many different ways.

In this chapter, I am thrilled to present a rich array of options that will empower you to nurture yourself, enabling you to uncover the true desires of your heart. You don't have to use every tool I will share in this book; you can choose. It's like a buffet. Keep it simple and add little moments in your day to try the practice of slowing down.

It also can be as simple as creating the space in your morning routine to enjoy your cup of coffee without distractions. It might be taking a short walk away from your desk to clear your head or spending a few minutes in the evening writing down the things spinning around in your mind.

I know firsthand how overwhelming it can feel to navigate through chaos and uncertainty and how easy it is to lose sight of your desires. But with these tools, you can gain clarity and direction that will ignite your spirit and give you the courage to take meaningful action toward getting what you want.

It all starts with a pause.

The Gift of the Pause

As we reach middle age, it's natural to reflect on our lives and question what we want for the future. This can be a time of transition and new beginnings. You may be launching your kids into the world, exploring a new career path, reentering the job force after caring for kids or aging parents, or finding yourself in another move to support your spouse.

Whatever the change, it can feel exciting. But on the other hand, it can also be an uncomfortable time filled with chaos, confusion, and uncertainty. You may grapple with questions like, "What do I want?," "What will I do now?," or "What comes next for me?"

Slow down and give yourself permission and time to pause.

Take a moment to recognize that you are a strong, capable woman with unique gifts God has given you. You've accomplished incredible things. You can and will handle whatever comes your way—the challenging and the easy moments. The most important thing you can do is accept the invitation to pause. No matter how difficult it can feel. Step out of the Messy Web and allow yourself to be still and quiet. Listen to what your heart and intuition have to say.

The thought of silence is scary for some of us. It was for me for years. There was a time when I didn't want to listen to my inner voice. The silence was so uncomfortable. I would let other distracting things keep me from hearing what I needed to hear. I would numb out by listening to a podcast, diving deep into a work project, or having the TV on without actually watching it. All to distract me from listening to myself. To avoid what was really at the root of it all.

I learned that this avoidance only perpetuated a sense of disconnection from myself and prevented me from accessing the wisdom and guidance within me. Learning to spend time in silence was a challenging practice that required patience and self-compassion. At first, restlessness and feelings of guilt would try to take over, pushing me to stay busy. I felt like I had too much to do to sit still. However, as I persisted, my body showed me that slowing down was okay.

Surprisingly, when I embraced the pause and surrendered, my mind cleared, my body felt less achy, and my thoughts became more positive. It was as if the fog lifted, and I rediscovered a newfound trust in myself. Embracing this daily pause practice revealed its benefits quickly. As I spent time praying, journaling, or walking in nature, I became happier, more balanced, and showed up as a better version of myself for me and everyone around me. The power of stillness had a profound impact on my overall well-being.

After learning this, I now know my body sends me signals and cues when it's time to pause and reconnect with myself. I know it's time to pay attention when I feel the tension in my shoulders, struggle to focus on what I'm working on, or my back aches from sitting at my desk too long.

It's time to put the pause into practice. In the stillness, in the moments of intimate self-reflection, I can genuinely find my truth and awaken to the clarity and authenticity that have been waiting patiently to be heard.

When we get comfortable with these moments of pause, sometimes listening to our thoughts and noticing our feelings can be rich with clarity and reveal our direction. We can hear the whispers of our inner voice, the part of us that knows what we truly want and need. Trust that your answers are inside you. Your inner wisdom knows.

Are there times in the day when you are giving yourself a chance to pause and listen to your inner voice? Or are you letting the distractions disconnect you even further from yourself and your body? This is not a time to judge yourself but to get curious, pay attention, and listen to what your body is trying to tell you. A pause can be powerful and healing.

Journaling

One of the ways to pause that my clients and I have found extremely helpful is journaling. Before you say, "I don't have time" or "I don't like writing," know that I used to feel that way too. I started a practice of journaling for just a few minutes a day and found it to be one of the most powerful tools for finding clarity in the chaos of daily life.

If you already practice journaling, I have some ways to make your journaling more intentional. Through this book, you'll have a chance to pause and find your answers with some of my writing prompts. This can help you make intentional choices and prioritize what truly matters to you, even when life feels like you are on a hamster wheel.

So, even if you only have a few minutes to spare, consider picking up a pen and letting your answers flow onto the page. You may be surprised by the insights you gain. Here are a few questions to help get you started.

Now It's Your Turn

What is it that you really, really want?
What would you do or change if you had everything you needed right now?
What do you want to accomplish in your life that you haven't done so far?

First, there are no right or wrong answers. Allow yourself to be vulnerable and open to exploring new possibilities. Don't agonize over answering. Write the first thing that comes to mind.

Second, no matter how impossible your answers may feel, there is a way. Our brains work hard to shape a reality that aligns with our beliefs and emotions. It's normal to feel uneasy with the unknown. You *can* gain control over your thoughts, allowing your intentions to manifest and come to life.

And finally, it's okay if you don't have all the answers right now. They will come. Instead of expecting immediate answers, embrace this time to explore and discover what you truly want and what matters most to you. Doing so will unlock the wisdom within you and help you gain the clarity you need to move forward with purpose and intention.

I mentioned journaling as a way to gain clarity. There are other ways. There are many different ways, like meditating, walking in nature, being creative with drawing or painting, or sitting quietly in prayer.

For Marie, who struggled with her move to Tampa, these questions became a catalyst for self-discovery. She gained clarity in articulating her desire to create her successful real estate business helping her clients find their ideal home. This opened her mind to the endless possibilities it would bring for her, her business, and the impact on her family. This newfound clarity allowed her to explore and decide who she wanted to become and her wishes, paving the way for transformative personal and professional growth. The pause is waiting for you. Give it a try!

The Art of Being

Chris had always been a doer, tirelessly taking care of everyone else. She felt exhausted and craving a change.

So, on our first coaching call, I asked her, "Who do you want to be?"

She seemed a little confused by the question, so I explained that, as women, we always jump into the "doing" in our lives. I wanted to know who she wanted to *be* and how she wanted to feel.

She answered, "I want to be a more kind, compassionate, and patient woman who feels more energy."

I then asked her, "Why is that important?"

Her shoulders slumped forward with a look of sadness as she answered, "I'm grouchy and in a rush most days, and my husband and kids don't always get the best of me."

"What kind of woman would you be if you were a more kind, compassionate, patient woman to yourself?"

As she spoke, her voice crackled, and her eyes welled up with tears. "I know I'll be a better wife and mom if I'm better to myself.

I want to be healthier, feeling more energy and joy by living in the moment."

We got to another critical piece in the pillar of clarity by discovering *who* Chris wanted to *be*. She did know her answer. And so began Chris' practice of living in the art of being.

Let me explain this. We're bombarded with messages telling us that we must accumulate more stuff, achieve more milestones, and continuously strive for more. It's exhausting, isn't it? And if that's not bad enough, what happens when we don't have the things or achieve what we want? Like when you don't lose enough weight, don't get that promotion, or don't get the dream home?

Our minds play a trick on us. We start thinking we're not doing enough, so we start doing more and working harder. We get fooled into thinking working longer hours will get us what we want or restricting ourselves will give us the results. We over-commit and begin to get into a vicious cycle that feels like we're on a treadmill that will not stop. We become addicted to being busy, so when we take the time to rest, we can't help but feel restless, like we must be doing something, or we feel guilty or lazy for just sitting still. This is why focusing on becoming the person you want to **be** transforms how you treat yourself and approach life, infusing it with love and self-compassion.

While it's natural to have desires and goals in life, it's powerful to approach them from a place of *being the person you want to be*.

This intentional approach allows you to connect deeper between your sense of self and actions. When you make choices from a vision of being the person you want to be and align them with mindful intention, you are more likely to achieve meaningful and fulfilling results.

Remember, it's not just about doing or having; it's about the journey of becoming. By intentionally creating your goals from your authentic self, you create a purposeful and fulfilling life.

Chris and I worked together in this practice each week to anchor in her new identity. Allowing curiosity to open the opportunity of how she could live into being who she wanted to be, I asked her during a coaching session, "What would it take for you to be a more kind, compassionate, and patient woman?"

That particular day lit a spark, and she smiled as she responded, "I would do something I enjoyed just for myself."

So we got to work! Through our coaching sessions, we worked on what that would look like and how it could be possible in her busy life. I encouraged her to ask herself "who she wanted to be" each morning before getting out of bed. As weeks passed, Chris started enjoying simple moments in her day, like a cup of tea in the morning, quiet time focused on reading her devotional, and short walks outside to enjoy the fresh air during her work breaks. These small acts of love for herself gave her the calm she was craving and rejuvenated her.

As a result, Chris found she had more energy and time for the things that mattered most to her. She realized that taking care of herself wasn't selfish but necessary to be the best version of herself. Chris no longer made taking care of herself a circumstantial choice. She relished the little moments that brought her joy and peace, understanding that she was taking action and living as her future self.

As you work towards gaining more clarity, take a moment to grab a pen and paper again. Allow your answers to flow from the most authentic version of yourself. Before diving headfirst into pursuing everything you want to do or have, pause and reflect on the following questions.

> ### *Now It's Your Turn*
>
> *Who do you want to BE?*
> *Describe how you will feel when you are that person.*
> *Who else will benefit when you are being the best version of*
> *yourself?*

As you answer these questions, know that **being** is about evaluating yourself with love and compassion. Take a closer look at who you are in the present moment and take small steps to be that future version of yourself. With it comes a powerful feeling that acts as a magnet to attract your desired outcomes. When you feel confident, trusting, or inspired, your actions reflect those emotions, and you begin to embody the person you want to be.

As Chris shared her weekly wins in one of our last coaching calls, she said, "I'm celebrating that I feel permission and freedom to ask myself each day who I want to be and how I want to show up. Then, I align my actions from that centered place. I know what's important to me and I now have the tools for keeping those priorities in place."

Chris embraced self-awareness and self-compassion, knowing she could better care for others by taking care of herself first. Chris is a shining example of the power of self-love, and living in the art of *being* helped her newfound ability to prioritize herself without guilt or hesitation. So take a deep breath, trust yourself, and allow your heart to guide you to be the woman you want to be.

Finding Your "Why"

Let me tell you about my client, Sarah. Sarah is a wife and a mother of three busy teens. She shouldered a substantial burden of family responsibilities due to her husband's demanding career as a physician. She rarely took time for herself, and when she did, she felt guilty. She believed her role was to be the caretaker for her family while balancing her busy career as a part-time accountant. As a result, she had difficulty saying "yes" to her own needs.

Sarah's busy life was taking a toll on her, and exhaustion was setting in. She raced through most days, eating breakfast while packing the kids' lunches and grabbing whatever food she could cobble together to eat at her desk as she worked through lunch. After work, she would race to pick up the kids from after-school activities, dash home for a quick change of clothes, and then off to soccer games. Many evenings, dinner was consumed on the go. She had little time to focus on any form of exercise. This reminded me a lot of how I used to live.

Sarah grappled with an "all-or-nothing" perspective in her life, believing there was no point in attempting if she couldn't work out or eat healthy with complete dedication. She sat at her desk for hours without any breaks and complained that her aches and joint pain had gotten more painful. She admitted how hard it was to feel rested because she never slept well.

When she'd lie down at night, her mind raced, making it difficult to fall asleep. Once she finally did drift off, sleep was short-lived, interrupted by waking up in a dripping sweat. She felt overwhelmed between her home responsibilities and work schedule. Her yearly visit to her doctor highlighted her fifteen-pound weight gain, and her blood work revealed her hormones were off balance. Her doctor declared she was in menopause.

Further blood work showed she was in the prediabetic range. Her doctor then made the statement that hit Sarah hard. "You will likely be on medication in six months if you don't make some changes and lose the weight."

Sarah was embarrassed and overwhelmed and felt a sense of urgency that it was time to make changes. This hit deeper than just the scale or lab report numbers. Her father had died from complications of diabetes earlier that year. This was her wake-up call.

Sarah's doctor prescribed hormone replacement therapy and referred her to a dietician for a nutrition consultation. Her doctor encouraged her to explore looking for a health coach because he understood that getting support and accountability would enhance her likelihood of success.

Sarah found me through the National Board of Health and Wellness Coaches website and booked a thirty-minute clarity call with me. We discussed several things, including her vision for her health, what she was struggling with, and the best way for her to feel supported. I knew Sarah had a strong why and our work together would be transformative for her.

At the end of the call, Sarah told me how different she felt. She felt hopeful and believed it might be possible to make some changes if she had someone in her corner to help support and guide her. She declared, "I need to be accountable for my goals because, if it's up to me to do this on my own, I know I won't do it." Sarah invested in a private twelve-week coaching program and we got started.

During one of our first weekly coaching sessions, I asked Sarah, "If you had everything you needed right now and nothing stopped you, what would you do?"

"I would have a plan for my day that included starting my morning with some intentional quiet time and a walk."

"What are your days like now, and what would you like them to be instead?"

"Right now, I race through my day, just living to make it to the end of the day. I have no intentional time for me anywhere in my schedule. I want to live more in the present moment and feel more calm and peaceful."

I could see her exhale as she was claiming this for herself. I asked her, "Why is it important for you to have a plan that includes time to feel calmer and peaceful?"

She replied with a look of sadness, "I don't want to end up like my dad, riddled with aches and pains. He lived his last years confined to his home and he was sick a lot. I want to be active with my husband and kids. I want to enjoy going to their activities, and I want to be around for my future grandkids. My kids don't have their grandfather, and it makes me sad to think I might not be around for my grandkids if I don't make some changes."

We were getting to Sarah's why.

As we worked together, she explored where she could make small changes to impact her daily life. After understanding how she wanted her day to begin, she prioritized changes in her morning routine. She set her morning alarm thirty minutes earlier. Sarah admitted she hit the snooze a few times in the morning, and when she did open her eyes, she would grab her phone and scroll on social media for at least fifteen minutes.

Now, she rededicated the first forty-five minutes of her day to herself.

Sarah started with quiet time, either in prayer or meditation, followed by a walk outside and a healthy breakfast. She was often worried she was wasting time with her new self-care habit. It became a battle of her mind. Family demands like kids' activities, grocery shopping, and laundry kept attempting to pull her away. However, our weekly sessions and communication between sessions helped Sarah stay accountable, and she quickly reset when I asked her to remember her why.

"I'm not breaking any more promises with myself," she said.

We continued to work on prioritizing Sarah's calendar, finding ways to remove things she wasn't passionate about, and delegating various things she needed to release. Through our conversation, she realized she wasn't communicating her needs to her family. She thought she had to do and be everything for everyone.

We often revisited her why to ground her in the importance of making these powerful decisions and communicating that to her family. We discussed delegating a few tasks to each family member. She also decided it was time to allow herself to hire some help with household chores, like cleaning twice a month and some painting projects that had been on her list for over two years. She gradually released the thoughts of guilt and the burden of controlling everything in her life to allow herself permission to ask for help and receive it.

As a result, her feelings of guilt began to dissolve. Sarah started noticing positive physical changes in her body, improved sleep, and her sense of being overwhelmed started to lessen. She felt lighter and happier, and her overall mood improved. Sarah realized how these changes positively impacted herself and everyone around her.

One particular day, when challenges seemed to mount up—kids needing rides, a pile of laundry, and dinner to be made—Sarah released the pressure to do it all. Instead, she delegated a small task to her husband and kids, allowing them to take responsibility.

She told me on her next coaching call, "All I had to do was communicate my needs. I could explain why I needed to focus on myself for my health. I will be no good to my kids or husband if I'm not around for them."

Creating a vision and setting intentions or goals are essential for success, but without a clear understanding of your underlying why, maintaining commitment can be challenging. Your why serves as the driving force behind your dedication, keeping you motivated and focused even when faced with obstacles.

Your why is an anchor, grounding you and reminding you of the reasons behind your actions. Imagine your life as a ship sailing on the vast ocean of possibilities. The anchor that holds the boat steady in the waves is your why, a solid and unwavering force that keeps you focused and grounded in your journey.

Let's take the time to understand and connect your why to your most important goal and set your anchor. Think of a goal you want to achieve and answer these questions to clarify why.

Now It's Your Turn

Why did you choose your goal?
Why is this goal important to you?
What will happen when you reach your goal?

Sarah's morning practice evolved into an unshakeable part of her daily routine. It wasn't just about the physical act of doing it but about the emotional and mental space it created for her. She cultivated a sense of peace and centeredness that carried through the rest of her day. But it wasn't always easy.

There were days, especially in the beginning, when she struggled to find the motivation to get out of bed or felt like the weight of the world was too much. In those moments, she had the anchor of her "why", why she had committed herself to taking better care of herself in the first place. It was about setting an example for her family and being around for a very long time as a healthy wife and mom.

As our sessions continued, Sarah noticed that she was more patient and more present in her life with her kids. Her husband noticed how much happier she seemed. He saw the connection when she started making time for herself and how this translated into a better relationship for them as a couple. She felt excited for her days again. She nourished herself in a whole new way by letting her why become the anchor when things were challenging and propelling her forward on her journey toward success.

Your Values in Action

I once heard a phrase, "When you are making any choice in life, decide as if you had Jesus walking beside you and your grandma looking over your shoulder."

It makes me smile because I loved both of my grandmas very much. They were my coaches in my life. I always wanted to make them proud. Although I may have made some choices that questioned that, their love never wandered.

I first heard this saying when my kids were teenagers. When I would have that mother's intuition that they were navigating tough decisions with friends, I would casually share that phrase with them. I prayed they had developed their values of doing the right thing even when it felt hard.

Do you have a quote, mantra, or scripture verse representing your values? You don't have to look far to find some powerful phrases. It might be noticing a sign at a local coffee shop, reading an inspiring book, seeing a persuasive quote on social media, or savoring the words of a meaningful devotional. Words have the power to represent our values.

Through furthering my education, I had the opportunity to take a values assessment during Compassion Integrity Training offered by the Center for Compassion, Integrity, and Secular Ethics at Life University.[1] It was an enlightening course that came at the height of the pandemic. This helped me realize that my values of honesty, love, spirituality, and leadership are my strengths which connected me to a deeper meaning and purpose in my life.

There are a variety of assessments to evaluate your values or strengths you can find through a simple Google search. However, one of my favorites is the Values in Action (VIA) assessment, a tool used in positive psychology to identify and measure an individual's character strengths and virtues. Created by Christopher Peterson and Martin Seligman, the VIA assessment aims to help people discover their unique strengths and values and apply them to various aspects of their lives for personal growth, fulfillment, and well-being. The assessment identifies twenty-four character strengths which are organized under six broad virtues that include:

- Wisdom: Creativity, curiosity, judgment, love of learning, perspective

- Courage: Bravery, perseverance, honesty, zest

- Humanity: Love, kindness, social intelligence

- Justice: Teamwork, fairness, leadership

- Temperance: Forgiveness, humility, prudence, self-regulation

- Transcendence: Appreciation of beauty, gratitude, hope, humor, spirituality[2]

One of my core values is my love for learning from the category of Wisdom. This value allows me to nurture my curiosity, better understand myself and the world around me. It empowers me to approach new situations with an open mind and actively seek opportunities for personal growth. Embracing my love of learning puts me in control of my personal development journey. You could call me a personal growth enthusiast. I find immense joy in participating in assessments or consuming personal growth books or podcasts to help me gain insights to further my strengths and values.

This assessment has taught me to celebrate my values and utilize my love of learning as a strength to become a better version of myself. In coaching, I use my passion for learning to help others discover more about themselves. This is why, after over three decades of working in different industries, I finally found what I wanted to be when I grew up! Reflecting on my life, it's clear how my love for learning has guided me through challenges and enabled me to thrive.

Your values are the things that matter most to you—the principles, beliefs, and ideals that guide your decisions and actions. When you live into your values, you tap into a source of inner wisdom that can help you navigate even some of your most challenging and uncertain times.

It's normal to feel a sense of loss or confusion and struggle with your purpose or meaning when you have a life-changing event. This might include but is not limited to things like a job loss or career change, a child going off to college, retirement, divorce, or the death of a spouse or parent. You can discover a profound sense of grounding and purpose by embracing and embodying your core values and celebrating your strengths. This foundation empowers you to navigate life's changes with increased confidence and clarity.

Emily's journey is a testament to the immense power of harnessing your values as strengths to create a life-altering transformation. When I first met Emily, her path was obscured by life's unpredictable twists, leaving her immobilized by the fear of the unknown. Emily had come to a crossroads of deciding to either stay in her current job as a financial consultant or take a leap and find a new job. She wondered if it was "too late" for her being in her late fifties. She felt defeated and trapped in a posture of negativity that permeated her workplace and strained her relationships with her husband and extended family. She was exhausted from the relentless hours of always being connected to her computer or phone for customer calls. She admitted she didn't know if she had the physical or mental strength to make a move. Emily grappled with the clichéd advice of thinking positively. Still, she knew through her previous experience working with a coach ten years earlier, she could regain her confidence and control of her life.

Through our coaching sessions, Emily's world gradually transformed. She learned the art of creating emotional boundaries, mastered the profound technique of reframing her thoughts, and embraced empowering mantras—a topic explored in greater detail in chapter 7, "Mindset of Saying "Yes" to Yourself."

The most pivotal session came when Emily and I reviewed her values assessment, uncovering her top five values. As we started the call, her excitement was palpable as we discussed her assessment report. Emily's top strength was hope.

She realized she'd always had hope in her life. Lately, though, she'd lost sight of it because of the external circumstances of her job and her strained family relationships. When Emily made the connection that this was circumstantial and it was in her power to use her value of hope to ground back into who she was, she gained clarity in seeing how her strength of hope was always there. She knew she could take control.

Emily reflected on her experience and said, "I had to shed the layers of negativity, and this coaching time has been a liberating space. The assessment and the revelation of my core values ignited my newfound pride. Positivity has surged to the surface, dimming the negativity."

After this discovery, Emily and I developed a plan for her to find a job that valued her skills and matched her values. We created an exit plan for her to leave her current position in finance. Emily found a new job that was a better fit for her work-life balance and where her expertise was recognized. With this change, she landed a job that allowed her to care for herself better, eat healthier by having planned meals, and spend more quality time with her husband.

As you gain clarity around your values, you can become more confident in setting boundaries and communicating your needs. You may seek relationships that are more aligned with your values and goals. It's an opportunity to become stronger, wiser, and more fully yourself.

> ### *Now It's Your Turn*
>
> *What are the values that are most important to you?*
> *How do you live your values in your daily life?*
> *How do your values influence your actions or relationships you have?*

Emily's story exemplifies the remarkable potential of aligning with your core values. She emerged from the shadows of defeat into a radiant realm of empowerment. Let her journey be a beacon as you seek transformation, underscoring that a life filled with fulfillment and joy is attainable with guidance, unwavering commitment, and self-discovery. Equipped with this wisdom, Emily is now on a mission—to reshape every negative into a positive each day—armed with the clarity gifted to her by the revelation of her value of hope.

Creating Your Vision

Now that you've taken the time to pause and explore what you want, think about why it matters to you, and what the values are that steer you, your intentional journaling has laid a strong foundation. This work has prepared you to begin forming your vision. It's time to take the next step and start creating your map for success.

Let's explore how the different parts of your life can come together to build your map for your future. The *Wheel of Life* is a valuable tool that can help you see how balanced and fulfilled you are. This is an opportunity to reflect on what is going well and what you would like to improve in critical areas of your life.

There are many versions of this evaluation tool available. For simplicity's sake, we will focus on five key areas: career, financial, spirituality, health, and relationships. I'll provide you with a few questions to answer so you can assess each area, understand what areas in your life are flourishing, and determine what areas need improvement.

While you explore these distinct areas of your life, remember that they are intrinsically intertwined, each profoundly influencing the others.

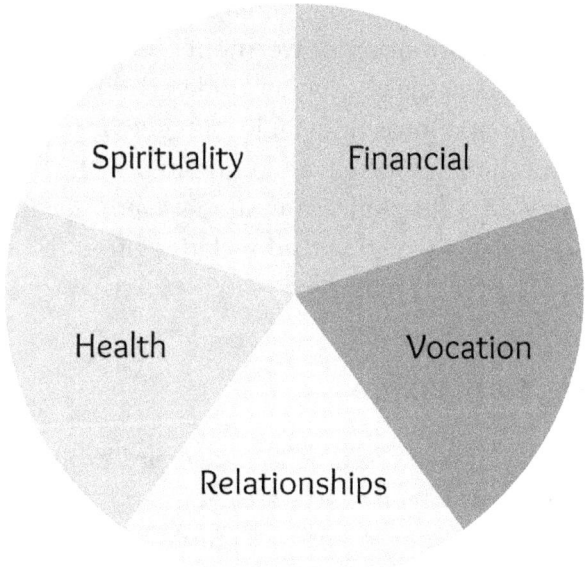

Let's first learn about each one:

Career

While the career area may seem obvious, this includes your chosen career, dreams, and personal growth journey within your field of work. It's not just about working, but a journey of personal evolution, finding genuine satisfaction and contentment in your work. It's about aligning your skills with your passions, shaping your career path, meeting your financial needs to support your lifestyle, and nurturing your personal growth.

It's about thriving in your role, striking a balance between work and your personal life, charting the course of your career progression, and addressing the obstacles that might surface in your professional path. This area isn't limited to traditional careers; it also encompasses areas like volunteer work, being a student, pursuing further education, or personal mission pursuits.

This is where you can plant the seeds of enrichment, nurturing your personal values, ambitions, and lifestyle preferences. Infusing your unique talents into your work creates a sense of fulfillment. Careful preparation becomes key by aligning your goals with the life you envision.

Now It's Your Turn

On a scale of 1-10, how satisfied are you in your career or vocation?
(A rating of 1 is dissatisfied, and 10 is extremely satisfied.)
What is going well in your career or vocation area of your life?
What actions could you take to be more satisfied in your career or vocation?

Financial

Navigating the realm of financial well-being requires a skillful and thoughtful approach to managing your financial resources. It's about adopting smart practices that let you live within your means and empower you to unlock your financial potential for a secure and prosperous future. This comprehensive journey encompasses various aspects, including managing your income, handling debt responsibly, crafting budgets, employing effective savings strategies, making informed investment decisions, and creating a solid long-term financial plan that considers elements like estate planning.

Striking a balance between your expenses, savings goals, and dreams for the future becomes the cornerstone of this aspect.

Achieving financial security isn't just about creating wealth; it's about gaining the freedom and flexibility to make life choices that align with your goals. This exploration involves practical strategies and a deeper understanding of how our emotions and perspectives impact our financial decisions.

This journey prompts you to explore your relationship with money—unraveling your views on scarcity and abundance and addressing the beliefs and emotions intertwined with your financial decisions. We each carry unique beliefs about money. The stories we have lived or created have significantly shaped our relationship with money. Finances can be an emotionally charged area of our lives.

Navigating your resources carefully involves ensuring your financial moves match your financial capabilities. It's about preparing for life's transformative moments, whether pursuing higher education, unexpected medical expenses, or retirement. As you tread this path, you're not merely crunching numbers; you're building a comprehensive framework that provides security, order, and readiness in the face of life's unpredictable twists and turns.

> ### *Now It's Your Turn*
>
> *On a scale of 1-10, how satisfied are you in your financial area of life?*
> *(A rating of 1 is dissatisfied, and 10 is extremely satisfied.)*
> *What is going well in the financial area of your life?*
> *What actions could you take to be more satisfied in the financial area of your life?*

Spirituality

Spirituality is a combination of practices, beliefs, and perspectives. While spirituality is often linked with religious doctrines, it can extend beyond organized religion's boundaries and take different forms. For some, the pathway to spiritual enlightenment flows through religious rituals, prayer, or the quiet practice of meditation. It can be a connection and belief in a higher power. Others might uncover it in nature's awe-inspiring setting or simple gestures of kindness and empathy.

It is a journey marked by the pursuit of finding calm and inner peace and discovering your connection in the world. The pursuit of spirituality involves the practice of mindfulness, introspection, and the nurturing of gratitude for the different experiences life offers.

It is a part of life that can be deepened with a heightened awareness, embracing your unique gifts and the interconnectedness with oneself, others, and the vast universe. It is about finding balance, even with life's complexities and uncertainties. Spirituality lends solace when tapping into faith and trust, even in the most trying times, offering a guiding light that extends beyond the ordinary.

> **Now It's Your Turn**
>
> On a scale of 1-10, how satisfied are you in your spiritual area of life?
> (A rating of 1 is dissatisfied, and 10 is extremely satisfied.)
> What is going well in the spirituality area of your life?
> What actions could you take to be more satisfied in the spiritual area of your life?

Health

When we think about staying healthy and improving our bodies, we often focus on diet and exercise. While nutrition and movement are important, there are other things to consider, like getting enough sleep, incorporating self-care activities to help promote rest, managing your thoughts and feelings, and dealing with stress. Developing healthy habits, enjoying exercises that energize you, and learning how to handle life's challenges can contribute to a healthier life.

It's essential to consider your mental, emotional, and physical health as interconnected. When evaluating your mental health, consider your thoughts and how you reason and evaluate things. It's also about having a practical mindset and being open to different perspectives. Your mind and thoughts are extremely powerful when you recognize how your thoughts are guiding your actions.

While mental health is about your thoughts, emotional health is about understanding and respecting your feelings. Understanding that your feelings are linked to what you believe, value, and know about yourself adds to your emotional wellness. Being positive, embracing who you are, and loving yourself all shape your emotional well-being.

> ### *Now It's Your Turn*
>
> *On a scale of 1-10, how satisfied are you with your health?*
> *(A rating of 1 is dissatisfied, and 10 is extremely satisfied.)*
> *What is going well in your health?*
> *What actions could you take to be more satisfied with your health?*

Relationships

Relationships are the emotional ties and connections we create with family, friends, partners, and colleagues. Healthy relationships result from a dynamic balance of effective communication, empathy, and a shared understanding, creating meaningful bonds that enrich our lives.

Within relationships lies the art of maintaining these connections, nurturing them, and fostering a well-developed support system. It's about cherishing the moments shared with loved ones and feeling the warmth of belonging in a community that resonates with your values.

In relationships, there's an art to keeping those connections strong.

It's important to learn how to communicate well. This involves sharing your thoughts and feelings openly, honestly, and empathetically. It also means engaging in social activities and your community, which helps keep connections alive.

Every part of relationships adds to our happiness, making us feel like we belong and sharing joyful experiences.

> ### Now It's Your Turn
>
> *On a scale of 1-10, how satisfied are you in your relationships? (A rating of 1 is dissatisfied, and 10 is extremely satisfied.) What is going well in your relationships? What actions could you take to be more satisfied in your relationships?*

Putting It All in Balance

By evaluating and giving each area a score (a rating of 1 is dissatisfied, and 10 is extremely satisfied), you can easily recognize where you're thriving and where you want to focus your efforts for growth. You can acknowledge your successes and nurture a positive attitude toward them while pinpointing areas that need attention and purposeful changes. This holistic perspective is a starting point on your journey toward a more balanced and satisfying life.

As you reflect on these five areas, answer these questions.

> ### Now It's Your Turn
>
> *What actions will you continue to take to maintain balance and satisfaction in the areas you've recognized as your strongest?*
>
> *What steps can you take to restore balance and enhance your satisfaction in the areas you've recognized need improvement?*
>
> *If you have multiple areas for growth, which one feels most exciting to focus on first? What is your top goal in that area?*

Let me tell you how this exercise helped Rebecca create her vision for something greater.

Rebecca was an ambitious woman convinced that her weight gain was solely due to her eating habits and lack of physical activity. As we did a version of this exercise, it uncovered a series of eye-opening revelations for her. A pattern emerged that she hadn't noticed before.

It turned out that Rebecca's focus in her life had shifted significantly towards caring for her elderly mother over the last eighteen months. The immense responsibility of attending to her mother's needs had gradually seeped into Rebecca's daily routine, making her feel unsatisfied and depleted. Mornings that used to begin with prayer, exercise, and nourishing rituals were now solely focused on driving her mother to doctors and other appointments.

Rebecca had relinquished her self-care practices while trying to balance everything she had taken on by being her mother's caregiver. The absence of her cherished morning routine had thrown her daily life into disarray. The added stress of caregiving had taken its toll on Rebecca's health and her relationship with her husband. They were having more disagreements and had not had a night out together as a couple in over six months. The once-strong bond with her husband was strained under the weight of the stress and changes that had crept into their lives.

As we dug deeper, Rebecca recognized the domino effect of her altered routine. The pressure had cast a shadow across three main areas of her life: her spirituality, health, and relationships. These areas had the most opportunity for growth. She felt undernourished in these areas and overwhelmed by how to even find time for herself.

Rebecca's story reminds us that our well-being is a web of interconnected threads. Sometimes, the root causes of our challenges are not immediately obvious and don't affect just one area of our lives.

By evaluating the different areas of her life, Rebecca learned why she felt so unbalanced and what was missing. This was a pivotal turning point for her. She began to find slivers of time she could claim for herself. Instead of listening to music on her commute in the morning, she would quietly drive in silence to clear her head and say a few prayers. If she was making calls in the afternoon, she would take ten minutes to sit outside in the warm sunshine between calls. After a long day of appointments, she parked her car in the garage and closed her eyes to take a few minutes sitting in silence with her eyes closed taking some deep breaths. She released the pressure to do it all on her own.

Enlightened with newfound insights from evaluating the different areas of her life, Rebecca began realigning her priorities in life by accepting outside help, focusing necessary time for her self-care practices, and establishing a biweekly date night with her husband. She reclaimed her morning routine by taking small steps to capture the little slivers of time, creating more balance and satisfaction in her life.

Let Clarity Be Your Compass

Thinking back to that moment during my husband's retirement ceremony when I finally allowed myself to exhale, I recognized the value of creating space. Space that lets clarity and new possibilities emerge. But in our fast-paced lives, finding that space can be challenging.

My journey to feeling more alive began with a moment of pause. Before that, I was caught up in the Messy Web of my life, giving away my time and energy until I was completely depleted. My relationships suffered and I missed out on the simple joys of life.

At the retirement ceremony, flashes of the future danced in my mind. Images of sitting on a warm beach, spending quality time with my husband, and enjoying moments with my kids vividly depicted what I wanted more of in my life. It was a stark contrast to my current reality.

This was my invitation. I realized I needed to stop, answer the call to take care of myself, and make room for the life I yearned for.

Creating space was challenging. But taking small steps to untangle the web did begin to stir the momentum I needed. It meant shedding the constant busyness and uncertainty that had defined my days. It felt uncomfortable to have no plan, but in that uncertainty, I let go and found freedom. I embraced the power to change things.

I made a bold move—leaving my job without a clear roadmap. But it was what I needed to do to release the stress and recalibrate my life.

Quitting a job may not be the best answer for you. There are always different options. Whether creating your exit strategy out of a less desirable position and into a new opportunity or creating your financial plan to support yourself through a transition like I did, there are always solutions available.

I spent precious time with my family, decompressed with my husband, and cherished moments with friends. This time-out, the space I gave myself, allowed me to see things differently so I could begin to build my plan that would nourish me in a whole new way, creating a life I wanted to live.

Getting clarity might be challenging, but it's worth practicing. As you go through different stages of life, getting clarity about what you want can help you feel more certain about your path. Taking time to understand yourself is a big step towards caring for yourself. It's like giving yourself a big hug. This journey is about discovering who you are and growing into the best version of yourself. It's time to answer the call within, and if something is keeping you from believing you can do that, we'll explore the most common beliefs that slow women down or keep us from saying "yes" to ourselves in the next chapter.

So, if you're a woman having difficulty finding your answers and feeling lost in all the noise, I invite you to pause. Let's appreciate the gift and power of reflecting and discovering the amazing things you can do. Believe that you can do it. The future is wide open with possibilities waiting for you. Allow clarity to serve as your guiding compass, leading you to rediscover the incredible woman you are!

Chapter 4 Key Takeaways

- Taking time to pause helps bring clarity to what you truly desire.

- Live by the art of *being* who you want to be instead of *doing*.

- Your "why" is your anchor, helping you stay focused and grounded for your goals.

- Your values are your strengths that show what you stand for.

- By exploring the five crucial aspects of your life—career, finances, spirituality, health, and relationships—with curiosity and an open mind, you can begin crafting a vision for what you want.

- Clarity is your compass to guide you on your journey.

I'm thrilled to extend a special invitation to you as a reader of *It's Your Turn*. Your journey with the book is just beginning, and I'm excited to offer you exclusive access to bonus resources and additional insights that complement the themes explored in this book. I believe that books are not just meant to be read but experienced.

If you would like to practice applying the *It's Your Turn* strategies to your own life, please use your cell phone camera to scan the QR code below or use the hyperlink at https://itsyourturnbook.com/resources.

itsyourturnbook.com/resources

Awareness of What's Slowing You Down

*Everything changed the day she figured out
there was exactly enough time for the important
things in her life.*
—Brian Andreas

As a guest speaker for a women's group, I was giving a talk about the importance of self-care and the value of rest. After my talk, an older woman, Janet, approached me.

"I wish I had heard your message four decades ago," she said. "If I had, I might have realized that taking better care of myself was worth my time."

I'll never forget Janet's words and how her body showed her life's wear and tear. When I sensed the regret and self-doubt that anything could be different for her, I recognized the limitations we often put on ourselves, especially as a woman.

Giving ourselves permission to care for ourselves can be challenging. It's common to feel trapped and need validation. Our beliefs and circumstances often significantly shape our thoughts and feelings, influencing our actions. Many women think we must put others' needs before our own, leading us to believe that self-care is selfish. However, it's quite the opposite.

When we prioritize our care, we recharge our energy and can experience a surge of excitement. This internal feeling activates those feel-good endorphins, motivating us to continue caring for ourselves. As we do this, we show up more fully and meaningfully for others.

When we take empowered action, this boosts our confidence and self-worth. Remember, no matter how far gone you feel about your physical health or situation, it's never too late to make a change that can positively impact your well-being. There is hope.

Have you experienced the excitement of starting something new? Going on a trip to a new destination, finishing a new exercise routine, getting a new job, moving to a new location, or even venturing into a new phase of your life, like being an empty nester? Unfortunately, it often doesn't take long before our minds sabotage our progress. Fear, doubt, guilt, insecurity, and uncertainty creep in, and our imagination takes over, conjuring up worst-case scenarios.

It's so easy to let these thoughts take over. Before you even begin, you might question your abilities, worry about potential failure, feel overwhelmed by the idea of getting started, or how you'll manage everything if you try.

Studies suggest it takes only seconds to infiltrate our thoughts and cast doubt on our abilities. If you find yourself in that frustrating spot where things aren't falling into place, you're not actively taking action on what you want, or you're feeling stuck, this is where I'll help guide you to recognize your beliefs that may be slowing you down.

In this chapter, we're moving on to the second step of the C.A.L.M. method: Awareness. This is about becoming aware of what's holding you back. We'll focus on something every person deals with: those self-limiting beliefs that can put the brakes on our progress. These beliefs are a tangled web of doubts and false stories that can easily convince us that putting our desires on hold is acceptable. But it's not.

Now that you've gained clarity to create your vision of who you want to be, defined your "why", explored the values that guide you, and learned how the connections of the five main areas of your life influence your well-being, it's time to learn more about what obstacles are slowing you down.

Let's first begin by looking into what could be the culprit behind a common symptom: procrastination.

What's Under Procrastination?

Discipline refers to the ability to control and motivate oneself to take action and complete tasks in a timely manner, even when faced with distractions or a lack of motivation. It involves setting clear goals, creating a structured schedule, prioritizing tasks, and developing habits that promote productivity. The killer of discipline is procrastination.

It's a common scenario: many women believe they lack the discipline to begin a new eating habit or exercise routine, take a well-deserved break, or have the most fit body. This belief of not being disciplined enough often contributes to feeling embarrassed, ashamed, or guilty. This can affect our confidence in whether we can do it, and we allow procrastination to take over, which often results in not making any changes.

I experienced this myself. I frequently relied on a particular phrase as a wife and mom dedicated to supporting her husband and family. Over time, I realized I used this phrase as a default response whenever I thought I couldn't take time for myself or go after something I wanted:

"I'll Do It When . . ."

- "The kids go back to school."

- "After we move."

- "My husband gets settled into his new job."

- "We have the money."

- "We get back from vacation."

- "I start my new job."

Don't get me wrong; stating this phrase is acceptable. But when I let it be the determining factor for anything that involved making a healthy choice that would benefit me, like taking care of myself, that was my problem.

Are you letting the "I'll Do It When" parade hold you back from getting started saying "yes" to yourself? There is more to it. The real culprit underneath procrastination often lurks in our minds. It's those sneaky self-limiting beliefs. They're like little voices telling us we can't do it, we're not good enough, or it's too hard. When one of those negative beliefs gets started, it is easier for others to join in.

But here's the secret: once we shine a light on these self-limiting beliefs and become aware of them, we can catch them in the act.

Awareness is your superpower. It lets you spot those self-limiting beliefs when they try to sabotage your progress. Instead of buying into their negative chatter, you get to decide what's true. We've been convinced of this negative chatter because we've heard it or experienced it somewhere in our lifetime. The reality is that when we are kind to ourselves, show ourselves some love, celebrate our strengths, and choose not to dwell on our limitations, those negative beliefs start to fall apart. There is no truth to them and they begin to crumble.

According to *Psychology Today*, procrastination results from various thoughts and habits that have us avoiding tasks or putting them off because we either don't want to do it, don't have a plan, or are unsure if we believe we can do it.[1] So, we need to ask ourselves three simple questions to understand what may be stopping us or what may be under our procrastination, especially when it involves taking care of ourselves:

- Do I really want to do it?

- Do I have a plan?

- Do I believe I can do it?

We can often explore these questions and find more clues to pinpoint the root cause or belief of the procrastination. For example, when we ask ourselves, "Do I really want to do it?" The reality is that this has everything to do with the reason you want your goal and your motivation behind it.

This goes back to chapter 4 where we learned the importance of finding your "why" and letting it serve as your anchor. If you want to achieve your goal and your motivation wanes, go back to your "why". Set your anchor again.

"Do you have a plan?" Having a plan doesn't mean that you have to do it alone. This could be an opportunity to look for someone or a community to help you create and implement your plan. We'll go into creating your plan in chapter 6, where you'll learn what you need in your personal plan to make it work for you.

Finally, "Do I believe I can do it?" There are many reasons procrastination shows up for us. But this question is one of the most powerful because this is where our self-limiting beliefs live.

Naming Your Self-Limiting Beliefs

The Gremlins was a terrifying film where these mischievous creatures wreaked havoc. I never watched the entire movie because it freaked me out too much!

Like those gremlins, inner gremlins can appear in our daily lives. Numerous names have been coined to describe these self-limiting beliefs, allowing for a creative selection like a gremlin, inner critic, superego, judge, saboteur, mean girl, critter brain, and inner bully. Each of these names represents the notion of negative self-talk and the internal havoc that undermines our confidence and potential.

You can name yours, and I'll stick with the gremlin for the example of self-limiting beliefs throughout this book. We can make this fun by personifying these gremlins and exploring them with curiosity to understand their impact on our thoughts and actions. Recognizing and addressing these limiting beliefs can help release the heavy pressure they place on us.

It's a choice to believe the story our gremlins are trying to convince us of. The stories we create about ourselves and others come from our upbringing, life experiences, and cultural and societal beliefs. Have you ever encountered a situation where something was said to you or by someone leading you to create a story or belief about yourself that wasn't true?

Of course, you have—we all have. We don't need to let these narratives dictate our life. We don't need to feel bad about ourselves because everyone has limiting beliefs. You are not alone, and I want to share some of the most common phrases that often come up with the women I meet who feel stuck in their lives.

- I'd love to care for myself, but I just don't have enough time.

- I could never get that promotion; I don't have what it takes.

- I don't think I will lose the weight because I've tried, and I'm not sure I can do it.

- I want to move more, but my body doesn't let me.

- I can't afford to do that for myself because we don't have the money.

- My life is too busy right now to care for myself.

- My husband won't ever change his eating habits so it will be tough for me.

- There is no time to rest; I have too much to do.

And then they get even more personal and nastier . . .

- What makes you think you'll succeed this time? You failed before when you tried.

- You tried to eat better last year, which lasted two weeks; why try again?

- Look at your long to-do list; you have no time to even think about taking a break.

- If you can't do it perfectly, why try?

- What makes you think you deserve (fill in the blank)?

- Who do you think you are?!

I could continue to go on and list even more. You may have heard or even said phrases like, "I can't do it" or "I'm not good enough." But the truth is that none of these statements are true. These beliefs aren't facts; they're just stories we tell ourselves.

Or it may have been something someone said to you, like a parent, teacher, coach, boss, coworker, or spouse. Either way, believing these stories can leave us feeling bad about ourselves, deflate our confidence, and keep us in our comfort zones. We may feel safe, but we're stuck because of these stories. These negative thoughts are like little gremlins in our minds, whispering doubts. I'm here to break these down and tell you they are lies.

So what do we do about them? First, recognize the gremlin when it shows up. That's right—call it out!

Second, you don't have to believe what the gremlin tries to convince you of. Accepting or unraveling these self-limiting beliefs is your choice to see they have no truth.

Third, instead of battling the gremlins, why not embrace them with kindness? These gremlins can be our guiding light, leading us towards something even more incredible for ourselves. Picture them as arrows pointing to areas that require our tender care and attention. In their unique way, they unveil what we need to shower ourselves with most: love and self-compassion.

Finally, take a different approach, do the opposite of what they say, or develop an empowering question that can help free you from believing it.

I had a strong gremlin for many years that told me, "You can't take time to rest." I grew up in a culture where hard work was rewarded, and I gained value through what I did. Others around me reinforced it and didn't know this added fuel to feed my gremlin.

I have learned to become friends with this gremlin. Rather than giving in or believing this gremlin when it shows up, I laugh and ask, "Who says so?" And then I ask myself, "How can I create time to rest?"

When I first did this, I had several ideas and decided what was suitable for me. I did that by asking myself, "What do *I* need right now?" My answers came, and I started taking action. I started by doing small things like taking ten minutes to do something relaxing. I did a quick meditation, took a short nap, or simply sat outside and enjoyed nature. Surprisingly, it worked wonders; the gremlin's voice grew quieter, and I realized how much better I felt when I took the time to rest.

Instead of fighting your gremlins, see them as messengers guiding you toward your blind spots and unmet needs. By understanding and addressing what they point to, you can quiet those gremlins down and tap into what you need to overcome the challenges of these self-limiting beliefs. You will feel calmer and more peaceful when you do. You do have choices. This is your chance to take your power back.

Treat yourself like you treat your best friend, especially regarding how you speak and think about yourself. It may require that you step out of your comfort zone. Your reward will be living into your tremendous potential. It's time to show yourself some self-love, compassion, and understanding.

Now, it's time for you to ask yourself some crucial questions. This will help you become aware of the stories you may have believed for far too long and allow you to break free from your self-limiting beliefs.

> ### *Now It's Your Turn*
>
> *What are your self-limiting beliefs that are slowing you down?*
> *What are your self-limiting beliefs trying to tell you?*
> *What action can you take to feel empowered to quiet your gremlins?*

Now that we've highlighted the potential barriers, let's explore the seven most prevalent self-limiting beliefs I've seen women encounter. These include thoughts like:

- "I don't have time"

- "I have so much to do"

- "I have to do it all myself"

- "I feel guilty for saying no"

- "I don't feel worthy"

- "I don't have the money"

- "I don't believe I can do it"

Additionally, I'll provide practical tools to help reshape these beliefs. You are invited to shift these limiting beliefs into empowering ones, fostering your confidence to motivate you toward being the incredible woman you were born to be.

"I don't have time."

I clung to the belief for years. In reality, I was causing chaos by not managing my time effectively. Despite raising my helium hand with my overcommit issues, I realized that making decisions was the root of my time shortage.

Surprisingly, one of the most significant contributors to our sense of time scarcity isn't our jobs, families, or health; it's our habit of wasting time by not making decisions efficiently. We frequently spend too much time procrastinating and deliberating, leading to needless delays and wasting precious time. This back-and-forth decision-making can also take a toll on our mental well-being.

We might believe we have no control over our circumstances, which can emotionally drain us even more. It can leave us feeling trapped and powerless. When we say, "I have no time," we reinforce that belief, and it soaks into every cell in our body.

Mastering efficient decision-making involves trusting our instincts while steering clear of the habit of overthinking, preventing analysis paralysis, and empowering us to take control of our time.

When clients express that they don't have time, it's an issue I empathize with deeply. Time is a limited resource, and there needs to be more of it. So, let's start creating more time for you. One of the ways to address this challenge is to understand how you currently use your time.

Keeping a time journal can be enlightening. This method lets you examine your day in detail, pinpointing how you spend your precious minutes. Once you know how you spend your time, you can decide how you want to spend your time in a future exercise I have for you.

By doing this exercise, you can liberate yourself from the belief of "I have no time" by taking a closer look at where and how you spend your time.

Now It's Your Turn

Here are the steps to create your time journal.

Step 1: Grab a notebook and decide what day you will start.
Start by defining the periods you want to track in: thirty or sixty-minute intervals. The choice is yours, depending on how specific you want to be.

Step 2: Begin with Day 1 by jotting down the time and record your activity for each designated time.
Be as detailed as possible. You can even track your feelings at different activities, which may provide even more clues. For example: Happy, tired, energized, focused, overwhelmed.

Step 3: Using a time journal for seven days can reveal more helpful information.
Record your times, activities, and emotions as you did on Day 1 for the next seven days. Try to stick as closely to your routine as possible. Being honest about logging everything you do will help you craft your new reality for how you want to spend your time.

Step 4: On Day 7, review your journal.
Take some time to go through your time journal for the past week. Look for patterns in your activities and emotions.

Then answer these questions:
Are there recurring patterns or themes?
Are there any activities that you spend more time on than you realize?
Are you noticing any open time gaps or time spent on mindless activities, like scrolling on social media or time that is unaccounted for?

Here are a few questions you can explore to dive deeper:
Are there times when you're consistently more stressed or relaxed?
Did you identify moments when you took time for yourself, even for a short time? Did this time affect your overall mood and energy level after you did it?
What things are clear that you want to change?
What will be your first action step to use your collected information to create more time for yourself?

The time journal is a simple yet transformative exercise that uses your curiosity as a catalyst to uncover insights into your current use of time. You may notice where time flows effortlessly and where it slips away unnoticed.

By understanding where your time goes, you can make conscious choices for yourself and have more time for the things you love. So, here's a new belief to reinforce this exercise.

Belief Shift

I use my time wisely by prioritizing what truly matters to me.

"I have so much to do."

Denise was a hard worker and always went above and beyond to help others, often sacrificing her time and energy. She had difficulty saying no to things, even when she didn't have the bandwidth to take on more.

Being raised by a single mom working multiple jobs, Denise strongly believed that she had to do it all, resulting in the phrase, "I have so much to do." This belief left her feeling overwhelmed, overworked, and stretched too thin. She often found herself inundated with last-minute requests at work, as her coworkers assumed she'd always step in to help due to her kind and accommodating nature. Family members frequently relied on her to organize family gatherings, often taking her willingness for granted. She admitted that her calendar was filled with commitments she wasn't very excited about that came from these requests.

Through our work together, Denise realized that her story of having to do it all needed to begin by changing the expectations she placed on herself and defining her boundaries. So, we started by clearing her calendar of unnecessary activities and prioritizing which ones mattered most to her. She decided to limit hosting family events to once a month to allow her sisters to share the load. She looked at her evening events and decided to cut the ones that didn't align with her position at work anymore. This cut it down to staying after hours one night every two weeks instead of two nights each week. It created open time with white space on her calendar.

As she began implementing these changes over a few weeks, she noticed a shift in her emotions. Feeling less rushed and calmer, she felt more in control of her life and less overwhelmed. Denise discovered the power of saying no to things that didn't align with her values and priorities, which resulted in saying "yes" to herself and her well-being.

She gained confidence that saying no was not a negative thing but a way to protect her time and energy. Denise transformed her belief from a woman with so much to do to one who could prioritize her needs and desires by being clear on her boundaries.

One way to feel less overwhelmed is by clearing the clutter in your calendar. Your calendar should reflect what matters most in your life, so look at what activities are filling up your schedule and prioritize accordingly.

Clearing the things that don't bring you joy will free up more time for meaningful moments that can offer peace and a renewed sense of happiness. If you are ready to establish better boundaries so that you feel more excited about what's on your calendar, you can use the *Priority Power-Up Practice* that Denise and I worked on in a session together. The *Priority Power-Up Practice* was designed to help you master saying "yes" and "no" and create better boundaries to release yourself from believing you have so much to do.

Now It's Your Turn

Here's how the Priority Power-Up Practice works.

Step 1: Start by pinpointing your top five priorities in life.
Write them down on a sticky note as your visual reminder. For instance, mine are spirituality, family (husband and kids), career, friendships, and health.

Step 2: Open your calendar and review your commitments.
While doing so, keep your top five priorities in mind. Ask yourself:
Does each activity or obligation on my calendar align with these
five priorities?

Step 3: When evaluating your commitments, determine if
you're a "Hell Yes" or a "Hell No" for each one.
If it feels challenging to answer, I ask, "Would I eagerly jump out
of bed to engage in that activity?" Notice your excitement or lack
of it when you do this step.

Step 4: Close your eyes and notice how the idea of that
commitment feels in your body.
Feelings have a profound impact on our body, influencing our
physical sensations. Positive emotions, like joy and contentment,
often lead to a sense of lightness and ease, while negative
emotions can cause stress physically, showing up as tension,
fatigue, or even pain. Does it feel expansive, or does it feel
constrictive?

Step 5: It's time to decide to eliminate the "Hell Nos" from
your commitments.
Letting go of these draining activities creates space for saying
"yes" to the things that will make a difference in how you feel.

Step 6: Keep the sticky note or take a picture of your Top Five
and place it somewhere visible on your calendar or phone.
Whenever someone invites you to join an activity, pause before
you answer and refer to your priorities. Does the invitation relate
to any of your top five priorities? If not, it's a "no". If yes, consider
how excited you are about it. Be sure it's a clear "yes".

> ***Step 7: With the "Hell Nos" cleared, you have room for the activities that resonate with your priorities.***
> *The energy and sense of relief of having an open schedule are undeniable. Having some breathing room feels incredibly liberating versus when our days are crammed with back-to-back appointments and tasks. This practice of self-discipline can empower you to make choices aligned with your values and what you want more and less of in your life.*

Now that you are putting the *Priority Power-Up Practice* into play, let's work on a new empowering belief to go with it.

> ### *Belief Shift*
>
> *I create balance and inner peace in my life by setting clear boundaries.*

"I have to do it all myself."

Mindy had an enlightening experience about the power of delegation. She had always been convinced that managing every aspect of her life was the only way. "I have to do it all myself," she often said. Then one day she confided in me, expressing her exhaustion and frustration with the relentless pace of her life. She felt burdened by the number of responsibilities at home, and to make matters worse, her company had just delivered the news that they were downsizing. Mindy was slated to take on additional duties alongside her current role. Something had to give.

I asked Mindy if she would take a few minutes and brainstorm to explore strategies to reduce her workload or help her manage her tasks. I reassured her that our exercise was a way to explore other options and she could decide if there was something she wanted to try.

She was open to it, so we started listing different ideas together. Things like involving her family members more in household responsibilities to help distribute the workload. There was the option to hire help for tasks like cleaning, lawn maintenance, or grocery shopping. We discussed the difference between critical tasks and those that could be postponed or eliminated. There was also the opportunity for her to talk with her manager about realistic expectations for her role at her workplace, especially considering the added responsibilities.

After we had a nice list, I asked Mindy, "Would you consider any of these options, and if so, which one might you want to try?"

She replied with a much lighter tone, "I think I could talk with my husband and son about helping with some things around the house."

"Great. Is there anything stopping you from having this discussion with them?"

Mindy hesitated. "Well, I'm not sure they will be on board with this idea."

Hearing the doubt in her response, we discussed strategies for having an effective conversation around this topic. So she decided to try it. One evening after dinner, she asked her husband and son if they could sit down and talk.

She told them, "I'm taking on more responsibilities at work and feeling pretty stressed about it. There are a few things around the house that I'm having a hard time getting done. I'm wondering if you could help me make a list to make sure I'm not missing anything and see if there is a way we can work on them together?"

Her husband and son were receptive and appreciated the open conversation. Together, the three of them created a list of tasks needing attention, like mulching the flower beds, completing two organization projects in the garage, clearing out a closet in their spare bedroom, and cooking responsibilities for an upcoming family event.

She asked, "I'm wondering if you would be willing to help with any of these?"

Her husband and son happily agreed and responded by choosing the ones that they knew they would enjoy the most. Mindy was shocked that they were both actually eager to complete the projects. They admitted they had noticed the tasks that needed to be done but didn't think she wanted their help. It turned into a surprisingly empowering discussion.

At our next coaching session, Mindy shared her wins for the week. After implementing this approach, Mindy realized she kept doing everything because she thought she had to. She had been holding herself back by not communicating her needs and asking for help from her family.

She said, "It was amazing and easier than I thought. I just needed to release the need to be in control of all of it and believe it was okay to ask for what I needed rather than doing it all myself."

Delegating tasks not only lightened her load but also strengthened the sense of unity within her family. A simple yet profound realization transformed their household dynamic and allowed them to work together more and give Mindy a chance to unload the heavy lifting she had been doing for so long.

Delegating tasks can be challenging, especially for women. It often stems from beliefs that we should be able to handle everything ourselves, a desire for control, or setting impossibly high standards for ourselves or others. Have you ever said any of these phrases?

"I'll just do it because it will be easier."

"I'll just do it because I can do it faster myself."

"I'll have to redo it, so I might as well be the one who does it right the first time."

There was a time when I did, especially as a busy mom with a demanding schedule racing from one commitment to the next. I found myself drying the dishes because they had homework, remaking the bed because it didn't look good, and loading the dishwasher because they wouldn't load it right. It's exhausting now just writing about it.

Reflecting on my past actions, I used to do this believing it would save time and not inconvenience my family. Eventually, I realized that by clinging to the belief that I must handle every task, particularly for my kids, I inadvertently denied them precious opportunities for personal growth, confidence building, and self-reliance. This revelation made it clear that my actions were causing me immense stress and overwhelm, a significant factor contributing to how my body reacted. This way of thinking and living contributed to my insomnia, gastrointestinal problems, and worsening hormonal imbalances, resulting in even more fatigue.

Allowing others to take ownership and make decisions is an opportunity to empower them and release yourself from the heavy burden you've been carrying. You might be thinking, *Will they really help?* The reality is that this is a learned behavior that we're permitting, as wives and mothers, with our spouses, kids, and coworkers. We've become accustomed to taking on everything ourselves, and others have come to expect it.

But as the saying goes, "nothing changes if nothing changes." Asking for help and delegating tasks may seem daunting initially, but this is a practice where you learn the power of delegation and release the belief that you must do it all. I call it the *It's the Who, Not You Practice* and it will make life better for everyone involved. Especially you! You can strengthen your relationships and help foster better self-sufficiency in your kids, spouses, and coworkers.

Things changed when I released the belief that I had to do it all, and I did it by applying the *It's the Who, Not You Practice* to my life. I didn't just do this in my personal life but also in my business. My clients admit it's one of the most liberating practices they have done in our work together. Try the practice.

Now It's Your Turn

Here are the steps and questions to start the It's the Who, Not You Practice to help you break that belief that you must do it all yourself, learn how to delegate, and free yourself to empower others.

Step 1: Identify what you can delegate.
These are the things that someone else can do. It's not you, no matter how hard you might try to convince yourself. What are the tasks, and who among my family, friends, and colleagues could I pass these tasks over to?

Step 2: Let others shine so you can live lighter.
These are the people who are your whos. Release the expectation that you have to do everything. You have capable people around you to empower and build their confidence. How can I leverage their strengths and willingness to lighten my load and create the opportunity for them to learn something?

Step 3: Be clear in communicating what you need and why.
This is where you get to practice asking for support. No one reads minds. Be clear and concise with gratitude. How can I be clear in asking and sharing my expectations positively and encouragingly to benefit everyone?

Here is a new belief to empower you while delegating.

Belief Shift

I release control of having to do it all, allowing and welcoming the support of others.

"I feel guilty for saying no."

I grappled with the weight of my obligations. I became acutely aware of the agonizing struggle to utter that two-letter word—NO. Saying "no" becomes an elusive, delicate art requiring relentless practice. My people-pleasing gremlin was obvious. The constant habit of saying "yes" and stretching myself thin took its toll, leaving me physically drained and simmering with resentment.

Saying "no" is often challenging because we prioritize the approval and validation of others. As a result, we fear rejection, experience guilt and self-blame, and struggle with setting boundaries. Overcoming this involves developing self-awareness, self-compassion, and assertiveness skills to prioritize our needs and well-being. Saying "no" is an essential part of maintaining balance and establishing healthy boundaries.

Now It's Your Turn

Here are three steps to learn to say "no" and release the guilt.

Step 1: Pause and assess.

When someone asks you for something or invites you to an event or commitment, take a moment to pause and assess the request. First, consider whether it aligns with your priorities, values, and goals. Then, reflect on whether saying "yes" would contribute to your well-being and happiness. Finally, ask yourself a few simple questions: "Do I really want to do it? Is this something I would jump out of bed excited to do?"

You may even notice how this feels in your body if you say "yes" or "no". Are you feeling excitement or does your chest feel tight or does your body feel tense? If you're unclear on an answer, give yourself twenty-four hours to consider it and see if your solution becomes more obvious with time. If that's the case, a good reply might be, "Let me check my schedule and get back to you tomorrow."

Step 2: Be clear on your response.

Once you've assessed the request and determined that saying no is your suitable decision, respond with a clear answer. This is not the place to be vague and left up for interpretation by others. Avoid going into lengthy explanations or justifications unless necessary.

Here are a few simple responses to try:
"I appreciate your invitation, but I won't be able to attend."
"I've checked my schedule, and it won't allow for anything new right now."
"I appreciate your invitation; it's not going to work for me at this time."

Step 3: Offer alternatives.

Depending on the situation, you can offer alternatives or compromises that show your willingness to help or participate without overextending yourself. For example, propose a different timeframe that works better for you, consider supporting the project financially, or connect them with another person or resource available to help.

You might feel enthusiastic about only some tasks, but being part of a family or community often comes with responsibilities. However, you have the power to establish boundaries regarding the amount of time and effort you contribute, ensuring that you can be helpful without overextending yourself.

Remember, saying "no" is essential for caring for yourself. When you say "no", you make room to say "yes" to yourself and the things that matter most to you. It might feel strange initially, but it will get easier as you practice releasing the guilt of saying "no".

Communicating "no" is the highest form of self-care. Here's your new belief to practice.

Belief Shift

I create joy and balance by doing what's best for me.

"I don't feel worthy."

My friend Margot told me an incredible story about her husband's thoughtful act. As a professional woman who became a stay-at-home mom for over fifteen years, Margot often struggled to feel her value because she wasn't receiving a paycheck and contributing to the family financially.

Sensing her unhappiness, Margot's husband wanted to help her see the immense value she contributed to their family. One day, he asked her to list everything she did for the family. He wrote it down meticulously, noting every responsibility she shouldered. Then, armed with this list, he diligently researched the cost of hiring professionals to perform each task and attached a monetary value to every item on the list.

When he unveiled his findings, Margot was shocked that the amount was significantly higher than if she had been paid for her full-time career work. It was triple what she'd reported in her last year of working outside the home. His purpose was not to diminish her efforts but to highlight her invaluable contribution to their family. He wanted to help her realize that her unwavering dedication and relentless efforts warranted acknowledgment, and her value far exceeded what she was currently giving herself credit for, regardless of any monetary compensation.

Margot's husband displayed unwavering compassion and support in that profound gesture. He acknowledged that she felt undervalued. It's a reminder that many women, particularly those who have paused their careers to raise their families, relocated due to a spouse's job, or cared for elderly parents, frequently grapple with acknowledging their actual value and self-worth. It's a common thought trap that can be challenging for others to understand unless they have experienced it firsthand.

Many women silently bear the weight of the invisible load, an intricate web of responsibilities and emotional labor that often goes unnoticed and unacknowledged. The stress and balancing act of managing household chores to tending to the emotional well-being of their families remain hidden despite their significant impact on daily life. It's time to shine a light on this invisible labor and give credit where it's due. We may not receive a financial paycheck for the many things we handle daily as a wife and mom, but it doesn't mean what we do isn't valuable.

Embracing a strong sense of worthiness is the cornerstone of self-care for women. It's a vital factor that can make navigating change challenging, influenced by our internal beliefs and external pressures. The connection between feeling valued and our innate sense of worthiness is undeniable. Acknowledging our value has a transformative effect on our self-perception and how we interact with the world. This unshakable sense of worthiness empowers women to assert, "I deserve respect, love, and care."

With this newfound conviction, they prioritize self-care, understanding that by nurturing themselves, they become even more adept at nurturing those around them. Worthiness triggers a profound shift in perspective, fostering a cycle of abundant love and appreciation, ultimately leading to a more fulfilling life.

If you like what Margot's husband did, you could do the same powerful exercise to help you recognize the value you provide daily to those around you, not just from the doing in your life but who you are for everyone around you.

Now It's Your Turn

It's time to complete your "Recognizing Your Value, Unveiling Your Worth" audit. Here are the steps:

Step 1: List the responsibilities you handle daily for yourself and others.
Include everything, from household chores and caregiving to work-related tasks and personal commitments. Consider everything you do in the year; this can include a variety of things like planning the family vacation, scheduling the yearly maintenance on the home, calling the insurance company for adjusted coverage, and organizing records for taxes, etc. You do many more things in a year, so credit those too.

Step 2: Next to each task listed, research the cost if your family had to hire someone and write it down.
This is an estimate to show what value each task provides. This can be a general ballpark number.

Step 3: Now, add all the numbers.
This is just the beginning of your contribution to your family. Recognize the value you provide to your family and how much you contribute to your family is so much more than this number. Your worth is priceless.

> **Bonus Tip**
>
> *Consider creating this as a date night opportunity for you and your spouse to connect and appreciate each other. Each of you can make a list. Remember to let this be fun and easy. You may need to discuss the invisible load each of you carries.*
>
> *Be grateful for each other rather than having a conversation that could become very possessive, leaving both of you feeling angry, unvalidated, and hurt. When my clients have taken the time to do this exercise with their partners, they say it opens up deeper conversations and opportunities to feel more connected and closer in their relationship.*

This exercise can help you discover your tremendous contribution and the value of who you are and your efforts. It's a great way to gain a fresh perspective on your impact and the value you add to your family, work, and community. Let's reinforce your belief in your self-worth and value with a new belief.

> ### *Belief Shift*
>
> *I am valuable and worthy of love and respect.*

"I don't have the money."

Kelly's days were filled with the hustle and bustle of life, from volunteering at her daughter's soccer games to managing spreadsheets at her desk. Yet, despite her diligent efforts, there was one thing she believed she could never afford—going on a dream trip to Italy with her daughter as a class chaperone.

Kelly, a hardworking mother, always whispered the same refrain, "We don't have the money." It was a phrase passed down from her struggling parents. For years, Kelly had carried the weight of their financial worries on her shoulders. Her parents had struggled to make ends meet, and she had internalized their financial struggles as hers. It was a money story she had inherited that limited her dreams and kept her from believing she could have something more.

I understood that Kelly's "we don't have the money" mantra was not just a statement of financial facts but a profoundly ingrained story of her money beliefs from years of believing what she had lived.

We began peeling back the layers of her money story to get to its roots. Together, we uncovered some truths: spending less and earning more are two paths to wealth, and every decision on how we earn or spend money is a choice. So we began brainstorming and created a list of ways Kelly could cut her spending or make more money. Many ideas came up in our conversation, and we discussed options and which ones might be the best.

Then I asked a simple question that would make her pause—"Have you ever considered asking for a raise at work?"

Kelly blinked in surprise, her mind racing. She had been at her job for over three years and consistently proven her value to the company but had yet to receive a raise.

"The conversation at work is always about how we are watching the budget, so I was assuming a raise was not a question I could ask. But now that you bring it up, I have never considered *asking* for a raise. I've just been waiting for them to give it to me at the right time," she replied.

My question ignited a spark of courage within Kelly. We talked about strategy and developed her plan to stand in her value and ask for a raise. She left the call feeling inspired and hopeful. She scheduled a meeting with her supervisor, equipped with evidence of her accomplishments and a strong case for a raise.

During the performance review, Kelly's supervisor was impressed with her dedication and the results she had delivered. To her delight, he informed her that she qualified for a raise. Kelly left that meeting with a sense of accomplishment she hadn't felt in years. She'd shattered one of her long-held money beliefs, proving she deserved more. Kelly knew that to fulfill her dream of taking her daughter to Italy, she needed to have another courageous conversation, this time with her husband.

Over dinner one evening, she expressed her heartfelt wish to her husband and asked if they could figure out a way to make it happen within their family budget. With a shared vision and a commitment to making this dream come true, Kelly and her husband began to have a serious look at their budgeting and financial planning. They combed through their expenses, making conscious choices to reduce nonessentials, and explored opportunities to generate additional income.

Kelly's determination paid off. She reported that she had indeed received the raise she had asked for. With careful budgeting and decision, she and her husband had created a plan to have enough money to make the dream trip to Italy with her daughter a reality.

Kelly's work is a testament to the power of challenging deep-seated money beliefs. It showed that often, what holds us back from achieving our dreams is not our financial situation but the stories we tell ourselves about money. Through courage, determination, and a willingness to confront those stories, Kelly had not only transformed her financial reality but also realized that she could have the things she had once believed were out of reach. She was worthy of asking and receiving!

In America, the gender wage gap remains a persistent and troubling issue. Women earn less than their male counterparts for the same work. This gap reflects a stark compensation inequality and highlights systemic disparities in opportunities and career advancement. Society often links financial wealth to one's worthiness, associating higher incomes with tremendous success. When we lack financial abundance or face economic challenges, we may wrestle with feelings of shame and inadequacy, driven by the belief that our value diminishes due to our inability to meet societal expectations. Comparisons with others often exacerbate these feelings of unworthiness.

Our ideas about money are created through many factors. Family upbringing plays a significant role, as the values and attitudes regarding finances instilled in us by our parents and close circles shape our perspectives. Personal financial experiences, positive (like receiving rewards for hard work) and negative (such as financial hardships or debt), contribute to our money beliefs, influencing notions of abundance or financial caution.

External influences, such as media, advertising, and social platforms, also mold our views on wealth, success, and consumer behaviors. Access to financial education and the knowledge gained from it can further refine our understanding of money management, investments, and financial decision-making. Finally, our unique personality traits, like risk tolerance and impulsivity, can significantly influence our money beliefs and economic behaviors.

Our money stories are complex and influenced by various aspects of our lives, making it challenging to pinpoint a single solution for fixing our money beliefs. What's crucial is recognizing how these beliefs impact our self-worth and influence our decisions. There's no one-size-fits-all remedy for healing our money wounds, but the first step is becoming aware of when these stories, often rooted in fear and scarcity, drive our choices.

We must recognize that personal worth extends far beyond financial circumstances. We get to decide what money means to us and change the beliefs that we currently have about it. Money is a resource, a tool to allow us to provide the life we want for ourselves. We get to choose what we invest in for ourselves and our lives. We have to break the cycle of unworthiness and recognize that true self-worth is based on an individual's inherent value as a human being, our unique qualities, and our contributions to our relationships and communities.

Developing a sense of self-acceptance, focusing on personal growth and fulfillment, and cultivating supportive relationships can all contribute to a healthier perspective on self-worth, irrespective of financial circumstances.

Now It's Your Turn

Here are three steps to start recognizing your money stories to shift to abundance.

Step 1: Identify your current money beliefs.
Start by recognizing your existing money beliefs. Understand what thoughts or attitudes you currently hold about money, whether positive or negative. How do your beliefs about money show up in your life?

Step 2: Acknowledge the influence of your money beliefs.
Examine any positive or negative beliefs you may have about money. Where did these beliefs originate? How do you think they have influenced your current beliefs about finances?

> ***Step 3: Challenge and seek positive influences.***
> *Challenge any negative beliefs around money and consider alternative, more empowering perspectives. Surround yourself with positive influences related to money. Read books, listen to podcasts, and engage with individuals who have healthy and positive relationships with money. What steps can you take to shift negative money beliefs for a more positive outcome?*

Let's begin by creating a more empowering money belief.

> ### *Belief Shift*
>
> *I am abundant and get to make the choices to create the life I desire.*

"I don't believe I can do it."

In high school, I was an average student and earned good grades. Standardized tests were something I never took until my first and only ACT for college entrance. This was before prep courses and classes for high school students were available.

I did very little to prepare. I even worked a late shift with my job at McDonald's the night before. I woke up early and took the test in a cafeteria filled with students from neighboring schools. I knew I didn't do well as I felt mentally exhausted as I handed the packet to the proctor. Some weeks later, I sat down with my school guidance counselor after receiving the scores.

"With these scores, you probably won't get into college," he said, looking over his reading glasses at me.

Feeling embarrassed, shame rolled in like a dark storm cloud on a hot summer afternoon. Things looked dark and felt heavy. I could feel my chest tighten and my body shrink as I wiggled in my chair. Although I don't remember if any advice was given after that, my head started to spin from the uncertainty of my future that was flashing before me. Walking out of his office, I felt defeated and started questioning how smart I was and my abilities as a student. The seed of self-doubt was planted.

After that meeting, I realized I knew one thing for sure about myself. I'm a hard worker and determined to achieve any goal I set for myself. When something stands in my way, I rise to the challenge. So, despite the doubt looming, I applied to the one university I wanted to attend, visited for an interview, and got accepted. I was going to college.

I worked through college with a part-time job and then graduated with an associate degree in respiratory therapy. I did what I had to do and I was proud.

But I still had an underlying belief, a lie that started about myself when I sat across from my guidance counselor. Underneath my success was the story of self-doubt and questioning that would chip away at my confidence, resurface, and show up in different ways throughout my life. I didn't realize how much that twenty-minute conversation would impact me, but it did.

In coaching, we frequently explore how our beliefs can empower or constrain us. I've come to acknowledge that I believed I wasn't good enough, which chipped away at my confidence. This led to a habit of questioning myself in various situations.

Shortly after graduating college, I took another standardized test for my respiratory boards in 1991 and missed passing it by just a few points. I believed I wasn't good at taking standardized tests—another hit to believing in myself and my abilities. However, I rolled up my sleeves, studied harder, retook the board exam, and passed. I remember not feeling confident walking in or out of the test that day. But since I did pass, I brushed it off, continued working as a respiratory therapist, and enjoyed that work.

In 2019, I decided to take the exam to become a National Board Certified Health and Wellness Coach. My experiences from my other standardized tests brought up feelings of self-doubt again.

This time, I recognized the thoughts and emotions flooding in because of my experience training as a coach and working with clients. I spotted my self-limiting belief. I was intimidated because this test was the highest credential health coaches could earn.

My memories flashed back to my ACT and respiratory board test experiences. My lack of confidence and doubt in my abilities had me on a roller coaster of emotions. One day, I would feel great and full of confidence; the next day, I would give all my excuses for being unable to do it. I knew the actual work I needed to focus on was the story stopping me from believing I could achieve this goal.

Recognizing what held me back made me understand the need to break down my old beliefs and approach the story from a new perspective. So, yes, I had to study the material, but I also knew I had to work on believing I could do it and change my thoughts and beliefs about it. I took action!

I asked myself, "What would a person who passes the test do?"

First, I put structure, routine, and accountability into place to help me pass the exam. I invested in and joined a weekly study group program and connected with an accountability buddy, with whom we agreed to check in once a week. Support through being involved in the community and accountability were invaluable.

Second, I created a study plan to fit into my busy life and scheduled it on my calendar as a visual reminder. This was my appointment with myself, and I was not allowed to break it.

Third, I practiced test questions to help build my skills in analyzing the questions and pacing myself during the test to help build my confidence in my test-taking abilities.

However, my most significant impact was how I treated my body and set up my nonnegotiable practices as part of my well-being care plan. I got serious with looking at my calendar and made some decisions about what was a "yes" and a "no" for me. I communicated with my husband and kids about my plan, how I needed their support, and what help I needed from them to reach my goal. They were supportive and were my biggest cheerleaders.

I delegated household tasks like assigning nights for cooking dinner, helping with household chores, grocery shopping, and lawn work. This all created more study time. I added a self-care plan of moving my body and meal planning to be sure I was fueling my body to perform at my best. My calendar became my visual cue by setting reminders in my electronic calendar and phone. My mindset work became part of my daily workout, like moving my body. I immersed my brain with positivity, inspiration, and programming to recreate my beliefs about myself and my abilities and release my old beliefs.

I started listening to a daily podcast called *The Bible in a Year with Father Mike Schmitz*. As I was driving to the testing center the morning of the test and listening in, his last sentence was a message for me that I knew was more than a sign: "You do your best, and God will do the rest."

It reminded me to exhale, and I could feel the difference in my body and confidence. I did my best and now knew it was okay to trust myself and the practices I had implemented to achieve my goal. With my plan and God's help, I crossed the finish line. I passed the exam the first time!

The way we boost our confidence is by taking action. The key to unlocking a world of possibilities is believing in yourself. Inside you, there's a well of untapped potential, just waiting to be discovered. You have a unique mix of strengths, talents, and experiences, making you unique and capable of achieving great things.

You're qualified, worthy, and deserving of all life's good things. Embrace your individuality because there's no one else quite like you. Now is your time to believe in yourself because, through belief, you unlock your path to greatness.

Now It's Your Turn

Here are three steps to help build your belief in yourself.

Step 1: Reflect on your past successes to build confidence in your abilities.
Start by developing a deep understanding of yourself by identifying your strengths and acknowledging your accomplishments. It reminds you that you have overcome challenges and can do so again.

Step 2: Use your positive feelings to fuel new goals.
Reflecting on past achievements boosts self-esteem and provides a roadmap for success. The emotions tied to past successes can be powerful catalysts for achieving current goals. The joy, pride, and satisfaction from those successes serve as motivational fuel for pursuing new goals.

> **Step 3: Break down larger goals into smaller, more manageable tasks.**
> *Harnessing these positive feelings can propel you forward, helping you approach current goals with determination and believing in your potential for success. Achieving smaller goals provides tangible evidence of your capabilities, fostering a sense of accomplishment and building confidence in your ability and trust in yourself to tackle more significant challenges.*

Try this new belief to build your confidence.

> **Belief Shift**
>
> *I believe in myself by embracing opportunities to build my confidence.*

Breaking Free from Self-Limiting Beliefs

As we close this chapter, you might recognize a few limiting beliefs within yourself. We went deep into the heart of self-limiting beliefs and their direct connection to procrastination. While many such beliefs exist, we've covered just a handful that commonly slow or stop us from taking action. These invisible barriers have been holding us back from unleashing our full potential.

But here's the powerful truth: By cultivating self-awareness and recognizing the sources of these beliefs, whether they stem from our upbringing, life experiences, or societal pressures, we gain the strength to confront and reshape them. As we unravel this intricate web of beliefs, we clear the path for transformative and personal growth.

Take Janet from the beginning of this chapter. Her story of regret for not taking better care of herself reminds us that we all confront moments of regret and self-doubt. However, we need to remember that change is always within reach. Instead of dwelling on the past or fearing the future, I want you to hold onto hope and know there is an opportunity for you to achieve what you want.

Fueled with these fresh beliefs, you can put these empowering stories into action as you learn what your body needs to flourish. It's time to seize this opportunity and unleash your full potential. Remember, "YES, YOU CAN!"

Chapter 5 Key Takeaways

- Procrastination is a sneaky, self-limiting belief.

- Self-limiting beliefs can stem from your upbringing, life experiences, or societal pressures. They are not true and they are stories we've believed.

- Creating awareness of your self-limiting beliefs is the opportunity to rewrite new narratives to liberate yourself. The antidote is action to reinforce your new belief.

- You get to choose how you spend your valuable resources of time and money.

- You get to create space to say "yes" to your needs.

- Recognizing your value shapes a healthy sense of worthiness.

- Cultivating self-confidence and believing in your abilities helps navigate challenges.

- You are worthy and you can do it!

If you would like to practice applying the *It's Your Turn* strategies to your own life from this book, please use your cell phone camera to scan the QR code below or use the hyperlink at https://itsyourturnbook.com/resources.

itsyourturnbook.com/resources

Chapter 6

Learning to Listen to Your Body

Listen to your inner voice for it is a deep and
powerful source of wisdom, beauty, and truth, ever
flowing through you.
—Caroline Joy Adams

One Friday evening, with John deployed to Afghanistan in 2012, the house buzzed with our usual routine. I juggled preparing dinner for the kids, tackling piles of laundry, and submitting my online homework for my bachelor's degree. As the clock ticked past 8:00 p.m., I realized I hadn't received our usual Friday night check-in phone call. A feeling of unease grew.

I went to the computer and pulled up my email. That's when I saw the Yahoo headline banner: "Afghanistan Base Under Fire." It was his base. A sudden rush of fear, worry, and an overwhelming sense of powerlessness came over me. I knew the military's standard protocol in situations like this was to cut off communication with the outside world to ensure the safety of everyone involved. However, that knowledge didn't make the situation any less nerve-wracking. As the minutes ticked by, my mind began to fast-forward through a litany of worst-case scenarios. My body tensed with each one. My concerns grew about what John might be dealing with as one of the medical providers. Different images of chaos flashed through my mind.

I had to stop myself. I couldn't go down that dark path. My two young kids were in the next room. I had to hold it together.

I reminded myself that my husband served alongside some of the most highly qualified service members. Relying on my faith in God, I closed my eyes and said a quiet prayer. But the stress weighed heavily on my body, my emotions held in check, all for the sake of being strong. I couldn't let myself cry or show how scared I was in front of my kids. I avoided turning on the television, fearing the news media might break in to share another heart-wrenching story of the war and the lives lost. I didn't want our kids to be reminded that Dad was in an unsafe place. I didn't need the reminder either.

I kept busy for the next thirty-six hours to stave off the anxiety. As we went through our weekend, the kids and I worked on homework and did some household chores. I tried to keep things as normal as usual. On Sunday morning, we went to church. I felt the comforting presence of God holding me. It was good to be around people in our faith community, even if no one knew what was happening in our lives.

After mass, we strolled through downtown Annapolis to browse the shops and grab lunch. As we walked around, I tried to ground myself by focusing on the trees changing colors from green to yellow and orange. Despite the beautiful fall scenery, I felt numb.

We had lunch at one of our favorite places. I kept my cell phone close, ensuring the ringer was turned on so I didn't miss a call. I would casually sneak a peek at my email when my kids were distracted, hoping they didn't notice my obsession with my phone. I didn't let my mind wander because I knew I would end up in a murky place. My body ached, my head hurt from not sleeping well, and I didn't have much of an appetite. My focus was to stay strong and just keep going.

As the waiter brought our check to the table, my phone buzzed and an email notification from my husband popped in. "I'm okay. I'll call as soon as I can."

As my muscles started to release, I felt my shoulders drop as I let out a big exhale.

That was all that I needed. For that day.

During that demanding time, I was juggling an unrealistic load—a full-time job, the responsibilities of a mom, the weight of being a single parent, and the pursuit of an online bachelor's degree, topping it all off with the emotional weight of worrying about my husband. I often wonder how I managed to do it all. We had no immediate family nearby to help with the day-to-day juggle of commitments. I had supportive coworkers, some with family members in the military, and a few trusted friends I knew I could reach out to if I was in a bind. Despite that, I never asked for help. I was just doing what I needed to do.

As I layered more stress on with my daily activities, I wasn't allowing my body much downtime to process or purge my emotions. I kept it inside so no one, especially my kids, would think anything was wrong. I held it all in—tight. My hyper-achieving ways convinced me I didn't have the time. But my body needed rest and was trying to get my attention by sending signals. All I had to do was listen.

It began with subtle whispers of discomfort, like achy muscles, tension in my shoulders, occasional headaches, and indigestion. My thoughts raced, my focus wavered, and I hopped from one task to another. I was too busy to pay attention to the signals, too engrossed in juggling all the balls. I was denying my body what I needed most: rest.

The more stress I took on, the more fuel I added to the fire. Those ignored whispers from my body eventually grew into a thunderous roar. Later that year, I had the doctor's visit I mentioned in chapter 2, with the feeling of marbles in my throat, insomnia, palpitations, and irregular periods.

It took years for me to realize the consequences of chronic low-level stress and my relentless denial of rest. The emotional and physical weight during those demanding years caught up with me. As my stress was building, I was in denial. I kept thinking I could just keep handling it. I didn't want to appear weak. I put an incredible amount of expectations on myself. When I hit that wall of exhaustion near my husband's retirement, I had no choice but to start paying attention to my body. It was the beginning of finding my way back to myself.

As I began to change my relationship with Time, I also had to change my relationship with my body. The journey began with looking for ways to reduce my stress. I had to learn to do less and give myself more time to rest, much like what we discussed in chapter 5. In my quest for rest, I realized that my body held the answers, and my intuition guided me toward ways I enjoyed slowing down and decompressing. I'll share the different ways to find your best practices for rest in this chapter.

I found the intriguing connection between stress, hormones, and those crazy sugar cravings. I discovered the importance of consistent nourishment through intentional food choices. These were foods made in nature, free from processed sugars and additives that had been causing my digestive issues. Discovering the right foods for my unique body felt like accessing a secret key to unlocking my metabolism, giving me a newfound sense of energy. This motivated me to be more intentional about creating a plan for consistent nourishing meals, realizing that I was saving time, money, and mental energy when I did.

I learned that clearing clutter in my environment was more than tidying up. It helped me organize my surroundings and clear my mind. My relationships improved as I focused on caring for myself, recognizing how strong social connections can make a remarkable difference in my health. I changed my approach to exercise by becoming curious about how I could enjoy moving my body and be excited to do it, leaving me feeling more alive and energized. I also discovered that getting good sleep had many different solutions; most of all, it involved clearing my mind and letting go of emotional and mental baggage.

But the answer that truly transformed my life was giving myself permission to rest and taking the time I needed for it. Rest changed everything.

Whether you've just started to notice your body's signals or feel you're too far down the road, I'm here to offer hope that there is a path forward. Things can get better. In the pages ahead, you'll discover the craft of listening to your body—a skill often underestimated in the chaos of modern life. We'll dive deep into the impact of stress on our lives and the necessity of understanding how it affects every facet of our well-being. Chronic low-level stress can infiltrate your daily life and doesn't discriminate. We'll explore the importance of managing stress, decluttering your environment, and the power of strong social connections. You'll also discover the significance of meal prepping and balanced nutrition, the role of regular physical activity, and the rejuvenating effects of quality sleep. And finally, most importantly, how to prioritize rest.

No matter your circumstances or the busyness of your schedule, you can take control of these aspects of your life. You might see the many things I explore in this chapter and feel overwhelmed. It's important to remember that I took my journey one step at a time.

I began by selecting one specific area I wanted to focus on, and I started there. I encourage you to do the same—choose the aspect that excites you the most. Try just one thing for one week and observe how it unfolds. Embrace curiosity and release judgment! Attempting too many changes simultaneously can be challenging. That's why it's best to initiate with a single change and gradually build from there.

Once you've mastered that first habit, celebrate and then introduce another. This incremental approach is not only more manageable but also more motivating. Small successes will inspire you to take on the next exciting challenge. The ultimate purpose of this chapter is to equip you with the ability to recognize the signals your body sends, understand what you need to nourish yourself, and take actions that work for you. Your health and life depend on it.

Unraveling the Impact of Stress on Your Health

According to the findings of the October 2023 *Stress in America* survey, women reported higher levels of stress than men and were more likely to rate their stress as severe.[1] Women expressed feeling less understood and having difficulty getting over their stress. The survey also revealed that women were more likely than men to be consumed by money-related stress, family responsibilities, and relationship stress. These are pieces of the invisible load and part of that Messy Web.

Women often struggle with acknowledging and coping with stress and are more likely to internalize it, which can lead to both physical and mental health issues. None of this may surprise you. It doesn't me. But it's reassuring to know that it has the attention of psychologists, who acknowledge the concern and emphasize the need for personalized wellness approaches.

The one-size-fits-all mental health strategy is not adequate given the diverse experiences and stress triggers among women. Adopting a holistic approach to optimal well-being is most effective, as chapter 4 in *The Wheel of Life* emphasizes. This approach considers five essential areas: health, career, finances, spirituality, and relationships. These facets are interrelated and have a significant impact on one another. Consequently, when we focus on enhancing one particular area, it can trigger positive changes in other areas.

According to The Centers for Disease Control and Prevention (CDC), six in ten adults in the United States are battling a chronic disease, with four in ten carrying the weight of multiple conditions. This epidemic places a staggering burden on our healthcare system, costing a mind-boggling $4.1 trillion annually.[2]

The standard approach of seeking quick fixes or relying heavily on medications must be revised to address these issues. A deeper root cause exists. The strains on our healthcare and mental health resources have forced consumers into a perpetual crisis response mode to their health issues. The current medical care system in the United States is primarily built to manage sickness, with little resources or time to promote overall holistic well-being. While some positive movement exists on the prevention side and alternative medical practices that focus on this, we have a long way to go to make changes in the larger population. With the complex landscape of medicine, patients often feel lost, disempowered, and overwhelmed, while dedicated medical professionals contend with high levels of burnout.

For far too long, we've relinquished the reins of our health to the medical community, hoping they would solve our health issues and our puzzle for us. We've become consumers of a quick-fix approach. We've placed considerable trust in external solutions, often overlooking the profound impact of our power and lifestyle choices. It's time to recognize that the key to empowerment lies in our hands.

When we grasp the fact that we have the ultimate say in our health and wellness, we can reclaim our power and take deliberate steps towards a healthier and more fulfilling life. Our daily lifestyle choices hold immense power to shape our overall well-being and combat the onset of chronic conditions.

A 2018 study conducted by scientists at the Harvard T.H. Chan School of Public Health examined the impact of adopting five low-risk lifestyle factors on the health and lifespan of Americans. These factors included maintaining a healthy eating pattern, not smoking, engaging in regular physical activity, consuming alcohol moderately, and maintaining an average weight.

Results showed that individuals who by age 50 didn't adopt any of the five healthy lifestyle factors lived to be 79 years old for women and 75.5 years for men. However, those who adopted all five healthy habits lived significantly longer, with women reaching an average lifespan of 93.1 years and men living up to 87.6. These findings emphasize the critical role of a healthy lifestyle in improving our longevity.[3]

Despite these findings, numerous studies reveal the challenges people face when trying to adhere to strict diets, exercise consistently, or maintain a healthy weight. We see this each year when New Year's rolls around, and we start declaring resolutions to lose weight, move more, or get healthier. Research shows that only 9 percent of Americans complete their resolutions, with 23 percent quitting by the first week of January and 43 percent by the end of January.[4]

Embracing change can be complicated and overwhelming, especially in today's fast-paced world with conflicting diet advice, impractical workout routines, and difficulty finding proper support. Past frustrations with failed attempts to get healthier can make this journey even more challenging. These obstacles can contribute to our self-limiting beliefs, as we discussed in chapter 5.

While focusing on nutrition and physical activity is a significant part of your health, it's equally important to consider other things such as stress management, quality sleep, strong social connections, your physical environment, and maintaining a positive mindset. It's not just about what we eat and how we move; it's all these other things combined. This was the case for me. I started by making small changes, like clearing activities off my calendar, getting seven to eight hours of sleep consistently, and scheduling time with friends. I took small steps, which made a difference in how I felt.

When handling stress and boosting your health, it's important to concentrate on what you can control. I gave you a few tools in chapters 4 and 5 to help create more time and better boundaries for yourself. These are established by embracing the thoughts and belief that you control your choices. What you focus on grows. Believe in yourself!

So remember, first, start with small, manageable steps that can fit into your daily life. Next, remember that what works well for one person might be different for you. It's all about carving your unique path. And finally, in this journey, knowledge and learning are powerful. When you learn to listen to your body, it's a pathway to getting connected back to who you are and what your needs are.

So let's first examine how the trifecta of stress, hormones, and sugar is interrelated for middle-aged women.

The Connection of Stress, Sugar, and Hormones

As women enter midlife, the mounting responsibilities of caring for our families, managing demanding careers, and nurturing relationships can lead to overwhelming stress, much like I described in the Messy Web in chapter 2. Unfortunately, in this whirlwind, time for ourselves often takes a backseat, and we unintentionally overlook our bodies' signals. Consequently, we may grapple with symptoms that appear out of nowhere, leaving us mentally drained and disconnected from our bodies. Recognizing how your stress and symptoms are connected can help you understand how to take steps to resolve balance in your body.

In the book, *Burnout: The Secret to Unlocking the Stress Cycle*, by Emily Nagoski and Amelia Nagoski, the sisters emphasize that unresolved or chronic low-level stress can harm our well-being. They point out that it's not enough to manage stress superficially, like lighting a candle and taking a deep breath. Instead, one must actively work to complete the stress cycle to fully recover and return the body and mind to a state of relaxation and balance.[5] For instance, you may feel your body shift into that relaxed mode after a refreshing walk out in nature, receiving a supportive hug, having a good cry, or creating a good sweat during a workout. They explain how you can complete the stress cycle with physical activity, relaxation techniques, social support, self-care, time management, and sleep.

Having some positive stress in our lives, like taking on exciting projects, engaging in challenging workouts, or embarking on new adventures, can enhance our resilience and overall well-being. On the flip side, constant, unrelenting, low-level stress, the kind that we never get a break from, can take a toll on our health.

This chronic low-level stress is a significant contributor to inflammation in our bodies. As ongoing stress dysregulates our body's stress response system, inflammatory chemicals that negatively affect our health are released. Hormonal imbalances, brain fog, night sweats, low energy levels, sugar cravings, and weight gain become frustrating obstacles that make it challenging to keep up with life's demands.[6]

Stress plays a significant role in our hormonal health. Stress, especially chronic low-level stress, can disturb the delicate balance of hormones in our bodies, impacting everything from our menstrual cycles to our mood and energy levels.[7] In response to stress, our adrenal glands release cortisol, a hormone that helps us cope with perceived threats and stress. Prolonged stress can result in chronically elevated cortisol levels, disrupting other hormonal systems that regulate body functions in nearly every system of the body.[6] This was the case for me; finding the right healthcare provider to help me navigate the changes was the support I needed.

It's essential to consult your healthcare provider for any concerns or symptoms you may be experiencing. It's important to advocate for yourself, and if you don't feel supported by your current healthcare provider, find a different provider who will listen and support you in your health journey.

You might be surprised to learn the connection between stress, sugar, and hormones. They are intertwined and significantly influence each other. This can be a vicious cycle. This hormonal imbalance often leads to cravings for sugary or high-carbohydrate foods as temporary sources of comfort or stress relief. When we indulge in sugary foods, beverages, or foods high in carbohydrates, our blood sugar levels spike, triggering a surge in insulin production. This constant fluctuation in blood sugar and insulin levels can lead to insulin resistance, weight gain, and an increased risk of developing conditions like type 2 diabetes and metabolic disorders.[8]

Hormones, sugar, and stress are the trifecta, so we must focus on stress. So what can you do to manage your stress? Listening to your body is like deciphering a unique language only you can understand. It's a skill that empowers you to decode your body's signals and respond appropriately, especially in times of stress and chaos. We'll cover food later in this chapter, but let's concentrate on three stress-management strategies, which I refer to as *B.A.U.*, which stands for *Breathe, Ask, and Unload*. You can give them a try when you're feeling stressed or overwhelmed.

Strategy 1: Take Some Deep Breaths

When my husband said, "It's Your Turn," and I exhaled, I realized I had been holding my breath and keeping my body in a state of chronic low-level stress for many years. Holding your breath is a natural response when your body perceives a threat or experiences stress. This is part of the "fight or flight" response, where your body's sympathetic portion of your nervous system prepares to react to a perceived danger, focusing only on survival. Holding your breath can be a way of bracing for impact. Your body communicates discomfort through stress signals, like shallow breathing and increased heart rate. This limits the oxygen flow to your brain and body, causing even more stress and discomfort. Chronic breath-holding is also known to exacerbate anxiety. Another vicious cycle!

Taking some deep breaths activates the body's relaxation response of the nervous system, which is the opposite of the "fight or flight" response. The parasympathetic system is responsible for "rest and digest" functions. Deep breathing activates and helps calm your body to shift into "rest and digest." When you take deep breaths, your lungs fill with more oxygen to circulate to your brain and other body parts, slowing your heart rate and balancing other functions, like hormones. This balances the sympathetic and parasympathetic nervous systems, helping you feel calmer, more present, and focused.

When you stop to take a deep breath, it's the first step in acknowledging your body's needs. By taking a few deep breaths, you are tuning into your body's language, recognizing the need to de-escalate stress, and giving your body the start of the relaxation it craves.

Strategy 2: Ask, "What Do I Need Right Now?"

Stop. Take three to five deep breaths and ask your body, "What do I need right now?" I like this question because it's like having a direct dialogue with your body. It lets you immediately focus on your needs, intending to take focus off everything that might be spinning around you. It's a way to get into the present moment. There are many ways to respond to this question. There are healthy responses and not-so-healthy responses. Our answers tend to be how we have learned to cope with stress. There was a time when my response to this question was caffeine, sugar, or alcohol. Over time, I realized none of those things were helping my body. It was a harmful quick fix, not a long-term solution. Learning this technique was part of discovering who I wanted to be. I wanted to be the woman who learned healthier ways to respond and complete my stress cycle.

This question helps recognize and validate how you are feeling. Emotions are a way to tune into your inner wisdom. This takes practice, so don't worry if you don't find your solution immediately. It's like relearning how to listen to our bodies after years of neglect as if we're rebuilding a forgotten connection. The good news is that this strategy doesn't take much time, and when we begin to practice and listen, we can recognize what we need. It's not about focusing on past things that happened or worrying about what's needed in the future; you are in the present moment—listening and responding to what you need.

Do you need a quiet moment alone, a healthy snack, a walk to stretch your legs, or a hug from a loved one? Identifying your immediate needs allows you to address them, which can significantly affect your ability to regain focus. As we go further into this chapter, you can discover your favorite healthy answers by asking yourself this question. There are straightforward approaches that require minimal time and most don't cost a penny.

For this strategy to be effective, you must be honest with yourself. If you're struggling with addiction, I urge you to seek help from a qualified medical or mental health professional. There's no need to face this alone. Learning healthier coping methods is crucial to improving your overall well-being. Your journey to recovery can start today, and there's support available to guide you along the way.

Strategy 3: Unload Your Mind

In one of our sessions, my client Kelly said, "I'm having a hard time focusing." We had some foundational work to tackle before diving into her dream trip to Italy with her daughter, Kate.

Kelly was spread thin, juggling numerous daily responsibilities. Our first mission was to reclaim her time, which we did through the *Priority Power-Up Practice* we covered in chapter 5. She got a firm grasp on her priorities and delegated some specific tasks. Yet, in one particular session, she brought up another pressing issue: her struggle with sleep.

Kelly explained, "Every night when I try to fall asleep, I toss and turn. My mind races from one thing to the next. I have such a hard time getting to sleep."

"Tell me a little more about your mind racing. What are the things going through your mind?" I asked.

Kelly laughed and answered, "It's things like the grocery list, the things I need to buy for my mom's birthday party, paying the bills, my projects I need to get done at work the next day."

I imagined the flurry of activities spinning inside Kelly's head and agreed, "You do have a lot of things you are taking care of. I can see how that would make it hard to fall asleep."

Kelly had a tired look in her eyes as she said, "My mind just doesn't stop."

So I asked her, "What would it feel like if you could go to bed without all those things spinning around in your mind?"

"That would be amazing!" she responded with excitement in her voice.

"Would you be willing to try something for this week called a *Brain Dump* before you go to bed at night?" I asked.

Kelly eagerly responded, "I'll try anything if it will help me sleep!"

Your mind's chaos is a form of communication. It can be rather loud and distracting. It's easy to stay in a constant state of overwhelm and stress when you don't give your mind a chance to purge. Women's invisible load in that Messy Web is a significant source of mind clutter and stress. We can't expect to hold everything in our heads. Yet we try to do it, and it's exhausting and affects more than we realize.

An effective way to mind purge is a *Brain Dump Practice.* When you do a brain dump, you translate the whirlwind of thoughts into a language you can comprehend and manage. You respect your body's need for mental clarity and focus by externalizing your thoughts and writing things down. In today's busy world, many things can distract our attention and make it hard to focus. Notifications constantly bombard us, and so much information comes at us from many different directions. These distractions can be like thieves, stealing our attention and making it hard to feel focused and connected to anything in our present moment.

Mind clutter was a point of discussion between my friend Molly and me on her podcast, *Hire And Empower with Molly McGrath, Episode #194.*[9] Much like a junk drawer in our house, our minds often become cluttered with the ceaseless stream of responsibilities and tasks that saturate our lives. Unfortunately, just like that drawer, no matter how diligently we try to manage our thoughts, they seem to multiply and intertwine, leaving us spinning. We can carry things like people's birthdays, all the holiday tasks, the grocery list, the travel plans that need to be made, the car maintenance that needs to be scheduled, and the home taxes that need to be paid.

I could go on, but you're probably running your list in your head now. Our thoughts come from different places and mix, making a jumble of ideas and worries, leaving us overwhelmed and mentally exhausted.

But we don't have to live this way. As we dump these thoughts and prioritize, we create space for clarity and focus. By identifying and tackling the most pressing tasks, we alleviate the burden that weighs upon us, allowing for a sense of accomplishment. Our bodies feel the pressure released when we offload. Like neatly arranged items in our junk drawer, our thoughts become more accessible, enabling us to see and tackle each with intention and efficiency.

The *Brain Dump Practice* strategy worked for Kelly and many others. This is a simple practice where you can use a piece of paper and write down everything spinning in your head, then prioritize and delegate. It's all about making life simpler, not more complicated.

Here's how the *Brain Dump Practice* works.

Step 1: The Free Flow

Start with a piece of paper and a pen. The goal is to let your thoughts flow freely without judgment or structure. Write down everything that's cluttering your mind. There is no need to organize or format; just list all the tasks, commitments, and thoughts causing the chaos in your mind. Get it all out and write it down on the page.

Step 2: Prioritize and Release

This is where the magic happens. Look at your list and start categorizing and prioritizing. Divide your tasks into buckets and release what needs to be removed from your list and your mental load.

- Bucket 1: My Immediate Focus – These are the things only you can do and require your immediate attention.

- Bucket 2: Delegate or Hire – Identify tasks that someone else can handle. Delegating these tasks can relieve you of unnecessary stress.

- Bucket 3: Future Tasks – Determine which tasks can wait until next week or next month. Prioritize based on urgency.

- Bucket 4: Not My Business – These are tasks or commitments that don't belong on your list.

This is an exercise to recognize and remove the activities or things that have nothing to do with you.

This process prioritizes your tasks and brings clarity and focus. It quiets the overwhelming feeling of having to hold everything in your mind. After doing the *Brain Dump Practice*, here are some reflection questions for you.

Now It's Your Turn

Do you recognize a difference in how your body feels after doing a brain dump?
Do you feel lighter or less overwhelmed?
Does your mind feel less of the spin?

Experiment to find what works for you. Now you can use the visual reminder of the list to keep you focused. If you like that sense of accomplishment of checking things off, do it. You can reshuffle your list to what your priority is each day or week. Kelly frequently turned to this tool whenever she encountered difficulty focusing during her day or found her mind racing at bedtime.

Kelly came to her follow-up coaching call to share her celebrations, saying, "I've been doing the *Brain Dump Practice* each night before I go to bed for the last week, and I can't believe the difference in how I'm feeling. I drift off to sleep and stay asleep! I've even noticed how much more focused I am at work and get my projects done so much faster having my written list."

The *Brain Dump Practice* is a powerful practice to feel less overwhelmed and hone your focus. Now that you've created the beginning of your organized roadmap, you can ask yourself, "What should I focus on first?" These are the things in Bucket 1, Immediate Focus.

The beauty of this practice is that you don't need to keep everything in your head. Your brain dump becomes your external memory. So, the next time you feel the weight of an overflowing to-do list or your mind spinning, just grab that piece of paper and let the *Brain Dump Practice* help you reduce your stress and bring in more calm.

Learning to tune into your body involves more than just recognizing its signals; it's about respecting your unique needs and adjusting your actions to get your desired results. This relationship between your mind and body thrives on clear communication. By using *B.A.U., Breathe, Ask, and Unload,* you can understand your body's needs and reset to a calmer state.

Now that we've explored the process of decluttering our minds, let's shift our focus to how environmental clutter can affect our thoughts and feelings and explore ways to reduce the clutter in our surroundings to feel better mentally and physically.

A Clear Space Is a Clear Mind

Let's go to one of the most common places women wrestle with clutter: our closets. My client, Chris, shared how clutter in her closet made her feel overwhelmed and anxious.

"As I look at my clothes in my closet, I feel uninspired. My closet is unorganized, and I have clothes hanging in there that I haven't worn in years. It's a reminder of the weight I've put on over time too," Chris said with a look of defeat.

When entering her closet, Chris explained how she felt heavy in her body and spirit. She noticed her negative thoughts and admitted her closet clutter chipped away at her confidence and self-esteem.

"My closet is no longer a sanctuary but a chamber of anxiety, guilt, and discontent," Chris declared.

As we talked about how her closet and clutter were making her feel, the conversation turned when I asked, "What would you like to see in your closet instead and how would that make you feel?"

"I want a closet with beautiful clothes organized by the bright colors I love. I also want to know each piece of clothing fits me and makes me feel good inside," Chris announced.

As we discussed ways she could accomplish this, we began creating a plan for Chris to declutter her closet. Her pile of unused clothes grew as she put the plan into action over the next two weeks. She donated the outfits that no longer fit, making space for those that made her feel good about herself. She sold a few nicer items, which created some money to purchase a few new blouses and pants to add to her updated wardrobe.

On the following coaching call, she told me, "This decluttering project didn't just help my closet get lighter; my heart and mind did too. I felt like I was shedding the burdens of my negative thoughts and feelings with every item I cleared out."

As we talked more, Chris' sense of release was palpable. As she stood in her newly organized, uncluttered closet, she saw her physical space transform and felt an inner transformation. A renewed sense of optimism, motivation, and self-compassion emerged. Her body felt lighter, and so did her thoughts.

"The clutter in my closet has been replaced by a sense of freedom and empowerment," Chris said with a smile.

It's a reminder that decluttering is not just about tidying up a physical space but about liberating your mind and body from the disorganization and challenging experiences of the past. I wanted to share Chris' experience with you because it represents how clutter in your closet can impact your body's response and how eliminating that clutter can make you feel. Clutter, especially in places like our closet and the clothes we wear, can dramatically impact our emotional, mental, and physical health as women. The closet is just one place where clutter can show up.

Many other places in your physical environment can be transformed to impact your well-being positively. You can rearrange your pantry for easy access to healthy foods, clear out old paperwork, and organize your desk to create an environment conducive to work, joy, and relaxation. Simplify your sleeping space by removing excess items and decorations, which can create a more calming atmosphere. These decluttering steps can contribute to a more organized and happier living environment.

A cluttered environment can create obstacles to maintaining a healthy lifestyle and hinder our productivity and focus. The visual overload of clutter competes for our attention and makes concentrating on tasks challenging. The constant reminders of unfinished projects or misplaced items can derail our productivity, leading to a sense of overwhelm and inefficiency.

I experienced the heavy weight of physical clutter often with our military moves. The stacks of boxes and not knowing where anything was reminded me of the cycle of chaos every time we moved our family. A sense of relief and calmness would wash over me when we would get our home set up. Things like setting up the kitchen so we could cook meals for our family instead of relying on fast food or getting our bedrooms set up to get a good night's rest made a big difference in how we felt. Even today, organizing my office space helps me feel better prepared to serve my clients and run my business more efficiently.

Research has shown that a cluttered workspace can decrease productivity, increase errors, and cause difficulty maintaining concentration. When our surroundings are filled with disarray and chaos, it can affect our mood, emotions, and overall calmness. The accumulation of physical clutter is not just a matter of untidiness; it can generate feelings of stress, anxiety, and overwhelm that seep into other areas of our lives.

Chris felt this way every time she walked into her closet until we worked to clear her clutter. She took small intentional steps to clear and organize her closet. On a coaching call a few weeks later, Chris' words brought a smile to my face. "It's incredible how much lighter and happier I feel now, without that constant reminder of defeat from my cluttered closet. Clearing out those clothes that no longer fit me was more than a physical change; it was my permission slip to let go of the mental baggage I'd carried for far too long."

If the clutter in your physical space creates havoc in your mind and tension in your body, try the process Chris and I walked through to declutter her closet.

Here are the four steps you can take to help clear your clutter.

Step 1: Assess and Set Goals to Declutter

Take an honest look at each area of your home or workspace and identify the cluttered areas that require attention. Ask yourself about the purpose of each space and how you envision it functioning. By setting specific goals for decluttering each room, focusing on one area at a time, you can prioritize based on the level of clutter and its significance to you.

For instance, a kitchen might include a pantry, cupboards for glasses, dishes, pots and pans, drawers for utensils, silverware, spices, and a refrigerator and freezer. Pick one particular section and start there first.

Step 2: Visualize Your Space

Define your vision of an organized and clutter-free environment. Close your eyes and visualize how your space looks and feels, imagining the benefits it will bring, such as reduced stress and improved productivity. Consider how an organized space aligns with your values and supports you and your family. To keep your vision clear, write down detailed descriptions of how you want each area to be. You could even find inspiring pictures from your favorite home magazines, or Pinterest is a great place to generate ideas. This vision will serve as your motivation and guide throughout the decluttering process.

Staying with the kitchen, imagine what it would look like if the pantry was organized and stocked with items that are easy to find to whip up a delicious dinner. The pots and pans were easy to get to, and your dishes were beautiful, making you feel good when you had friends over for dinner.

Step 3: Set Goals and Priorities

Break down the process into smaller, manageable tasks you can tackle individually. Set specific goals for each decluttering session, focusing on a particular area of your home or a category of items. Consider setting realistic deadlines for completing each decluttering goal to maintain momentum and progress. Create a timeline or schedule, allocating dedicated time for each session by writing it in your calendar. For example, you may focus on the kitchen for one week, cleaning out the refrigerator on Saturday while concentrating on the pantry on Sunday.

Step 4: Pleasure Bundling: Tie the Task to Something You Enjoy

James Clear's book, *Atomic Habits*, has gained widespread popularity for its clear and actionable guidance on making long-lasting, positive changes through the power of small habits.[10] He explains a strategy called "Temptation Bundling." I like the phrase my coach, Sara Connell, introduced me to, which she calls "pleasure bundling." This strategy helped me write this book. This clever approach combines a less enjoyable task, such as writing, with a rewarding activity you love, making the entire process more satisfying.

While working on this book, which demanded numerous hours of writing—not something that comes easily to me—I needed a strategy to maintain motivation. I used pleasure bundling to help set goals for my writing, reach them, and celebrate. I would write for an hour, then go for a walk outside. I would write for a few hours in the morning, then have lunch with a friend. I would write for five days in a row and reward myself with a pedicure at the end of the week. And the craziest thing happened: I started enjoying writing even more. It worked! You have hundreds of hours of pleasure bundling in your hands as proof!

As we apply pleasure bundling to clearing out clutter, think about this. After spending some time decluttering and organizing a kitchen drawer, why not bundle it with a Netflix show you love? Once your drawer is tidy and everything is in its place, sit back, relax, and watch an episode of your favorite show. The satisfaction can make both experiences more enjoyable. It's like giving yourself a little energy boost on a job well done, turning a mundane task into a delightful moment of self-care.

You can decide that if you don't reach your goal, then there is no Netflix episode for that day. Feel encouraged to give it another shot the following day; employing this approach could motivate you to take it on. So give pleasure bundling a try on your next decluttering project or another activity or task you may not enjoy as much. It's a fun way to set goals, do the work, and celebrate you!

As we understand the connection between physical clutter and our mental and emotional state, we can recognize how this stress harms our bodies and health. It can motivate us to take action, create change, and reclaim a sense of tranquility in our lives. Clearing away clutter can help reduce the stress, anxiety, and overwhelm associated with it, making room for a more peaceful state of mind. Take it step by step, focus on one task at a time, and celebrate your achievements by enjoying some rest.

Now It's Your Turn

*Do you recognize clutter in your physical environment?
Does the clutter influence your thoughts or feelings in a positive or negative way?
What's one step you want to take to begin to clear your clutter?*

Answering Your Craving for Rest

During a heartfelt conversation with Mindy, she admitted, "I've always grappled with the idea that taking time for myself might make me look like I'm not a good mom. With no family nearby to help, I rarely do anything just for me, and it's hard to change how I think about it."

There's that Messy Web again. I must confess that I used to have thoughts similar to Mindy's. The societal stress of my beliefs led me to rarely allow myself to rest or invest time or money into my self-care.

But something incredible happened when I worked on allowing myself to prioritize rest. My family noticed a significant change as I started taking short walks to move my body, taking hot baths before bed, or closing my eyes for a few minutes in the afternoon. I became a happier and better mom and wife. I was more present in my life and theirs. I looked into my kids' eyes and stopped to listen to what they had to say when they needed something. John began to see the difference in how I felt. They got a much better version of me.

We spent more time doing activities together. I laughed and smiled more because I practiced gratitude, spending each morning in quiet prayer or journaling. I was moving my body and eating better. I was less distracted and more focused when my kids asked for help with homework. We had better conversations because I wasn't feeling so exhausted and wasn't in such a rush to get "everything" done. I was listening to my body and answering my craving for rest, and I showed up for others better because I took care of myself first.

In the hustle and bustle of our modern lives, rest often becomes a casualty, pushed aside in the never-ending pursuit of productivity and achievement. We find ourselves caught in a perpetual cycle of busyness, running on empty and neglecting the very thing our bodies and souls crave.

We've become a society that has let food, alcohol, tobacco, narcotics, overworking, social isolation, and excessive screen time, along with other unhealthy habits, soothe us or be a method of completing that stress cycle. And it doesn't work. We've lost our ability to learn how to cope and deal with stress in a healthy way in a world with so many demands and beliefs placed on us. It's as if we've been handed a beautiful, delicate flower, only to let it wither away under the scorching sun of our relentless stress.

It's easy to get caught up in the habit of constantly needing to do more and accomplish tasks, diving headfirst into a never-ending rabbit hole. This can leave us feeling unproductive, overwhelmed, and burdened with guilt. If we don't achieve the desired results, like reaching our exercise goals, meeting our weekly work obligations, or losing a few pounds, we think we have to work harder.

We'll discuss changing our mindset on rest in the next chapter, but just know that when we understand our thoughts behind the constant pressure to stay busy or that we can't rest, we can appreciate how to break free from that unhelpful way of thinking and be more intentional with our actions to show up in our life as a better version of ourselves.

Here's the truth: rest is the lifeline that breathes vitality back into our weary souls, rejuvenates our bodies, and rekindles our spirits. Without intentional rest, we risk becoming mere shadows of ourselves, running on fumes and fading into the background of our own lives. Taking time for yourself, like resting, is standing up for yourself. It's a skill that requires practice to become comfortable doing it.

It's time to listen to the whispers of our bodies and prioritize our well-being over the demands of a perpetually overscheduled life. Prioritize, fiercely guard it, and create nonnegotiable healthy self-care practices that honor your need for rest.

Rest is tuning into your body's unique needs. It's not restricted to a full night's sleep; it can be a few minutes of quiet time, deep breaths, or several hours of deep relaxation. There is no one-size-fits-all approach to rest. It varies from person to person and can shift throughout your day.

To truly grasp its power, we'll explore the various dimensions of rest, such as physical, mental, emotional, social, spiritual, sensory, and creative. I'll provide practical examples to help you identify what your body may be craving and ways you can respond. Discovering the restorative power of various forms of rest tailored to your needs is the key to comprehending how rest can revive and rejuvenate you.

Physical rest **involves giving your body a break from physical activity and allowing it to recover and rejuvenate.** It includes eating nourishing foods, getting enough sleep, napping, and practicing relaxation techniques like stretching or massage. Physical fatigue is often the first and most obvious sign of needing rest. It may indicate that your body needs restorative rest if you feel exhausted or lack energy, even after a good night's sleep. Looking for other clues such as difficulty sleeping, weight gain, weight loss, body aches or pains, digestive issues, or cravings are just a few physical signs.

Mental rest **is essential for calming the mind and reducing mental fatigue.** It involves taking breaks from intense cognitive activities, such as work, studying (writing a book), and engaging in activities promoting relaxation and mental rejuvenation, such as meditation, mindfulness, or hobbies. If you notice that your concentration and focus are diminishing or you are experiencing brain fog or having difficulty making decisions, it's a sign that your mind is tired and needs a break. Mental exhaustion can impact your productivity and overall mental well-being, so it's important to recognize these symptoms and take appropriate action.

I can feel my focus wavering when I've spent a long day on my computer. I love nature, so being mindful, taking short breaks to go outside, and using my senses help me recharge. I sit for a few minutes and appreciate the scenery, like clouds rolling across the sky or trees blowing in the wind. It's just one of the ways I give myself the gift of mental rest.

Emotional rest **focuses on acknowledging and honoring your emotions.** It involves creating space for emotional processing, allowing yourself to feel and express your feelings without judgment. Journaling, talking to a trusted friend, or self-reflection can support emotional rest. Emotional and psychological changes can also signal the need for rest, such as becoming more irritable, impatient, or easily overwhelmed. You may also notice decreased motivation and enthusiasm for activities you usually enjoy. These emotional and psychological shifts indicate that it's time to prioritize taking care of yourself. If I start to feel overwhelmed, especially if my negative thoughts get going, it's time to draw a bath and listen to soft music by candlelight. It slows me down and gives me a chance to reset.

Social rest **involves taking time for yourself and setting boundaries in your social interactions.** It includes seeking solitude, stepping away from social obligations, and engaging in activities that recharge you, such as reading, alone time, or practicing self-care rituals. Social rest can also involve nurturing and deepening connections with loved ones, friends, and family. These relationships provide a crucial support system and significantly influence our overall well-being. We create spaces of trust, love, and understanding by investing time and effort in fostering these connections. Sharing laughter, engaging in meaningful conversations, and participating in activities together allow us to build lasting bonds and find comfort in the company of those who know and accept us for who we are.

Recognizing the need for social rest often comes with cues from within. It may manifest as impatience or feeling short with others, a heightened sensitivity to being around people, a deep sense of loneliness, or a craving for human connection. Many of us became acutely aware of this need for social rest during the COVID-19 pandemic when isolation restrictions were placed on us.

Social rest may also be needed when you've experienced an energy drain from attending a conference or a social event. Advocating for yourself and acknowledging when it's time to say "yes" to your needs is essential. If we disregard these cues, we risk pushing ourselves into overdrive, depleting our energy reserves. This can lead to tangible consequences, such as fatigue, a weakened immune system, and other health issues. Remember, if you don't stop, your body might eventually force you to, like mine did. Listening to these cues and granting yourself the rest you need is an act of self-care that can lead to lasting well-being.

Spiritual rest **encompasses finding inner peace, rejuvenation, and a deep connection with oneself and the world around us.** It involves nurturing and tending to our spiritual well-being, which can take various forms depending on individual beliefs and practices. Engaging in activities such as meditation, prayer, reflection, or spending time in nature allows us to quiet our minds, center our thoughts, and find solace in the present moment. One of my favorite things is spending the first fifteen minutes of my day in a quiet house with a cup of coffee or tea, reflecting on what I'm grateful for. I may read a devotional or have dedicated prayer time to have a conversation with God. It starts my day with good intentions and prepares me for the day ahead.

By creating space for spiritual rest, we open ourselves up to introspection, self-discovery, and personal growth. This therapeutic practice enables us to detach from the demands of everyday life, find clarity, and gain a broader perspective on our purpose and values.

Sensory rest refers to giving our senses a break from constant environmental stimuli. Our senses can quickly become overwhelmed in today's fast-paced world, leading to sensory overload and increased stress. To achieve sensory rest, reduce sensory input and create a peaceful and calming environment. This can involve finding a quiet space free from distractions and noise, turning off electronic devices, and minimizing exposure to bright lights and screens.

Engaging in activities that provide a soothing sensory experience, such as taking a bath, listening to calming music, or spending time in nature, can also contribute to sensory rest. I enjoy declaring an occasional "tech detox" day where I shut my phone off and take a break from the constant barrage of emails, notifications, or social media scrolling. This promotes relaxation, reduces my stress, and restores balance to my sensory system.

Creative rest provides a space for our minds to wander, dream, and explore new ideas without the pressure of productivity or performance. It nurtures our imagination and allows us to tap into our creative potential. Engaging in activities that inspire creativity, such as art, cooking, writing, painting, sewing, playing a musical instrument, or immersing oneself in nature can foster a sense of freedom and exploration. During creative rest, we give ourselves permission to be unproductive and embrace the joy of free-flowing creativity. This process encourages us to let go of expectations and judgments, allowing new ideas and innovative solutions to emerge naturally.

When considering the most suitable form of rest for your needs, it's essential to recognize that there might be a combination that can offer a deeper sense of relaxation. Restorative rest, for instance, goes beyond merely stopping physical activity. It's a form of rest that promotes recovery and rejuvenation on multiple levels, including physical, mental, and emotional. Restorative rest is a more holistic form of rest that aims to restore and revitalize your whole self, not just your physical body.

When contemplating how to include various forms of intentional rest into your daily routine, here are four tips for establishing a consistent rest routine to help ease your stress.

Tip 1: Schedule Regular Breaks

Sprinkling small bites of rest throughout your day can help add some fuel to your tank. I like to call these "snack-size" rest breaks. There are several strategies when approaching this. You can set electronic reminders or use productivity apps to prompt you to take frequent breaks from work or other demanding tasks. Having a schedule where you preemptively schedule small breaks can be a way to help your nervous system reset.

Or you can do this on demand, asking yourself the critical question, "What do I need right now?" and then answering that question by actually doing what it is that you need. Use this time to relax and rejuvenate, such as taking deep breaths and listening to calming music, slowly enjoying a cup of tea, or taking a short walk outside.

Tip 2: Find What Works For You

Rest is a highly individualized concept, not a "one-size-fits-all" approach. Identify which rest and activities resonate most and incorporate them into your day. Take the time to explore the different types and determine what brings you the most relaxation and rejuvenation. Listen to your body's needs, try the activity you crave, and integrate these practices into your daily routine or whenever you need to unwind.

Tip 3: Embrace Leisure Activities

Spend quality time indulging in activities that light up your soul and provide that much-needed relaxation. These can be your hobbies, creative passions, travel, or leisurely pastimes that whisk you away from the daily grind.

Clients often confide in me, saying, "I can't remember the last time I painted, played the piano, or simply lost myself in a book just for sheer pleasure." Allowing ourselves these moments is frequently tied to our self-worth. Society can sometimes label us as lazy if we're not constantly being productive, which can take a toll on our self-esteem.

So, what's holding you back from enjoying some leisure time? If you're unsure where to start, try asking yourself: "What would I choose to do on a day that's entirely mine without the constraints of money, time, or permission?"

It could be as simple as diving into a good book, nurturing a flourishing garden, expressing your creativity through art, playing a musical instrument, sitting in the sunshine, or sharing heartwarming moments with friends or loved ones. These are the moments that will invigorate your spirit and nourish your soul.

Tip 4: Pre-Fill Your Rest Tank

When was the last time you took a nap? Scientists found that people who took short naps had better recall and cognition than those who did not. Preemptive rest is when you can strategically incorporate rest periods or restorative activities into your routine before stress or fatigue becomes problematic. This is a proactive approach to managing your physical and mental health to sustain productivity and overall quality of life. It's like topping off your car's gas tank before you make that long trip ahead.

One way the prefill strategy is helpful is when you know you will be around a large crowd of people or in situations that drain your energy. For instance, this strategy does wonders around the holidays when you know you have those extra festive parties for work, family, and friends, or you know you will be doing an activity that will take a lot of your mental and emotional energy. This may not just be naps. It may be meditation, prayer, or sitting outside, getting some fresh air. Give yourself permission for some quiet time to refuel and prepare for the time ahead.

Embracing different forms of rest allows you to restore balance, nurture your well-being, and create a sustainable and fulfilling life. By honoring yourself and valuing the power of self-care, you inspire and empower others around you to prioritize rest and reclaim their right to a well-deserved break.

One of the exercises I encourage my clients to do is to create their nourishment menu. This is your list of go-to activities you enjoy when you feel your body's fatigue and need replenishment. To create your nourishment list, answer these questions.

Now It's Your Turn

What activities or practices make you feel most relaxed and recharged?
How can you incorporate these restful activities into your daily routine?
What prevents you from prioritizing these restful practices?
How can you overcome them to create a consistent routine?

The Power of Strong Social Connections

One summer, my daughter Kaitlyn attended our church's summer camp in the beautiful mountains of northern Georgia. Since we were new to the community, this was an excellent opportunity for her to make new friends and see familiar faces on her first day at her new school.

As I listened to Kaitlyn's enthusiastic description of the camp, I mentally vowed that if the opportunity presented itself, I would attend. The following year, I was a parent volunteer for the youth group. I was fortunate enough to receive an invitation to serve as a parent chaperone, and I eagerly accepted.

The camp offered many exciting activities, such as white-water rafting, rock wall climbing, hikes to the local waterfall, prayer and reflection, small group sessions, daily mass, and the much-anticipated mud day. Mud day reminded me of field day in third grade, only with more entertaining and advanced obstacle courses and games, including a mud pit that became a highlight for all participants, parents included.

The entire week was a rejuvenating break from the everyday pressures of life. With little Internet access and a "no phone" policy, it allowed the time to meet new friends and reconnect with our faith and relationship with God. It was no wonder that the kids cherished every moment. I sure did.

During the camp, I partnered with another parent volunteer, Amy, to support a small group of freshmen girls, with the camp counselor taking the lead. Amy and I didn't take long to realize our shared passions: devotion to God, faith, and love for coffee.

Once our unforgettable week at summer camp had concluded, Amy and I decided to meet up one Friday morning to get to know each other better. Given that our family had only been part of this community for about a year, I was enthusiastic about the prospect of fostering new friendships with other women.

We met for morning mass and then savored a cup of coffee at the local Starbucks. We talked about everything we were balancing as women, the struggles and the celebrations with our families. The time together and our conversation lifted our hearts. We left with a vow to do it again the next week and invite others. What started as a casual gathering became the seeds for a new group of special friends.

Our small group quickly expanded as we wanted to spread the joy of these moments to even more friends. Our Friday morning gatherings became integral to our weekly routine. We began our day by attending 8:15 a.m. mass at the church, and after, we'd head over to our nearby Panera or Starbucks. Over cups of steaming coffee and breakfast, we'd share stories, laughter, and sometimes even tears. This wasn't just a typical Friday morning routine but a profound way to deepen our connections with other women going through similar things. It provided a space for us to grow in faith together while basking in the warmth of each other's company. One of our friends affectionately named our group "Jesus and Java."

The pandemic brought significant changes to our group's dynamics. Despite restrictions, we managed to stay connected. Adding to the complexity, Hurricane Sally struck our area in the fall of 2020 causing substantial damage, including knocking out the main bridge between Pensacola and Gulf Breeze, a crucial lifeline for many commuters. This led to extended commutes, transforming the usual fifteen-minute drive into a two-hour ordeal for locals. We were dealing with a triple whammy of challenges: a pandemic, hurricane damage, and transportation disruptions. Still, our group faced new challenges as things gradually returned to normal and schedules shifted due to various demands with kids going to college and other life changes.

While our group may look different today, we've managed to maintain our strong bond by keeping our group chat active. Despite each of us having our unique struggles, we have remained in touch primarily through text messages. We let each other know when we can make it for our Friday morning tradition. We receive regular invitations to join one another for meals, walks, holiday parties, and community events. It's also been a prayer chain for the special requests when we need prayer power.

These gatherings are more than simply sipping coffee. They represent a recharging of our cups with friendship, faith, and a profound sense of belonging. Our "Jesus and Java" group of friends epitomizes the strength of social connections within a tight-knit community. These weekly meet-ups underscore that our friendships aren't just casual interactions but the lifelines that bind us together. They remind us that, regardless of life's hurdles, our community of friends and family enriches our lives in countless ways, including living longer.

The *Stress in America 2023* study by the American Psychological Association highlights the profound impact of the collective trauma caused by events like the COVID-19 pandemic and other societal challenges.[11] It emphasizes the importance of social connections and their role in addressing the ongoing posttraumatic stress many are experiencing. While daily life may appear more normal on the surface, psychologists warn that posttraumatic effects have taken a toll on mental and physical health. This widespread trauma encompasses not only the pandemic but also global conflicts, racial injustice, economic issues, and climate-related disasters. Recognizing how ongoing stress can lead to inflammation and various health issues is critical.

In 2023, the US Surgeon General issued a warning in a report titled, "The Surgeon General's Advisory on the Healing Effects of Social Connection and Community," about how loneliness and isolation can seriously harm people in our country. Loneliness and social isolation can have severe consequences for our health, increasing the risk of premature death by more than 25 percent. To put this in perspective, lacking social connections can be as harmful as smoking up to fifteen cigarettes a day.[12] Loneliness is linked to increased stress, anxiety, depression, and dementia.

This impact isn't just psychological; it can also show up physically, increasing the risk of heart disease, obesity, and weakening the immune system. The absence of social connections can intensify feelings of disconnection and despair. It also leads to economic costs, with an estimated $6.7 billion in excess Medicare spending due to social isolation among older adults. Moreover, loneliness and isolation negatively affect academic and work performance, costing US employers an estimated $154 billion annually due to stress-related absenteeism.[12] So, staying socially connected is about well-being and reducing health risks and economic burdens.

Our connections with family, friends, and community contribute to our health. These relationships provide emotional support, encouragement, and a sense of belonging. They bolster our mental and emotional resilience as a buffer against stress and its adverse impacts on our well-being. Our social circles often guide our behavior, influencing our dietary choices, exercise habits, and lifestyle decisions. The advantages of solid social connections are abundant.

Numerous studies have shown that people with robust social networks tend to live longer, enjoy improved mental health, and experience reduced stress. Such individuals often exhibit better adherence to health-promoting behaviors, leading to lower rates of chronic diseases. The emotional support derived from these relationships can help us navigate life's challenges and provide a sense of purpose.

Given these insights, fostering and nurturing our social connections can enhance our relationships with family, friends, and the community, leading to positive health transformations. Connecting with like-minded individuals can profoundly enrich your life.

Now that you understand the importance of social connections, look back at the *Wheel of Life* exercise in chapter 4, under the Relationships section, and see how you rated yours. If you're looking for ways to strengthen your relationships, here are some ideas to consider.

- Explore local clubs to meet others in person.

- Participate in a class to learn a new hobby or skill.

- Get involved in events and gatherings in your area.

- Join in-person or online support groups or classes.

- Attend professional events to expand your network.

- Volunteer and meet like-minded individuals.

- Prioritize quality time with friends and family.

- Reconnect with friends you've lost touch with.

If social anxiety or mental health challenges make it difficult to connect with others, getting support from a licensed therapist is a crucial step. A therapist can offer guidance and strategies to help overcome these barriers, ultimately leading to a more fulfilling social life.

Now It's Your Turn

Who are the people or activities that bring you the most joy and sense of connection?
How do you currently maintain and nurture these social connections in your life?
Are there challenges preventing you from connecting with others?
What steps can you take to overcome them?

Consistent Nourishment with Meal Planning

Gloria's days were nonstop, and her life was a frantic blur. As an elementary school teacher, she raced to meet deadlines, cared for her family, and squeezed in social commitments. Her days were planned down to the minute, and her energy was a constant roller coaster.

When things got too intense, she turned to quick energy fixes like sugar and caffeine to get through the day. She admitted that she never really took the time to make a plan for her meals. She might grab a piece of toast or a bowl of cereal with a cup of coffee for breakfast. Lunch was a few carrot sticks, a protein bar, or a meal from the school cafeteria.

After her school day ended, she would make a quick stop at the grocery store, picking up a few items as she raced up and down the aisles, or she'd grab fast food at a drive-thru. During the school year, she and her husband would attempt to sit down for dinner, but often, Gloria would stay late at work to prepare for the next school day. By the time she made it home, her husband had already had his meal and was off to do chores around the house. Most evenings, she ate fast food or cobbled a few things together to make a meal from the refrigerator while grading a pile of papers or cleaning the house. She had no plan in place for meals. She felt the weight of exhaustion, yet she pressed on, convinced she had no time or way to do it any differently.

Over the last few years, Gloria had slowly put on extra weight. She reached a tipping point when she started experiencing periods of extreme exhaustion that made it difficult for her to make it to the end of the school day. She decided it was time to see her medical provider.

After a physical exam with a comprehensive blood work panel, her doctor revealed that she had an imbalance with her hormones and blood sugar level. Her doctor gave her the choice to either try making some habit changes and lose some weight or start medication. She encouraged Gloria to find ways to handle her stress better but knew it wouldn't be easy.

Gloria felt she owed it to herself to try to make some changes and didn't want to rely on medication for the rest of her life if she could prevent it. Gloria's doctor, aware of my work with her other patients, recommended she seek my support. Within a few days, we had a call and were working together. Gloria was ready to get started.

With my guidance and support, Gloria focused on taking simple steps to slow down. We discussed what needed to happen for her to start.

"I need a plan that includes managing my stress, eating better, and moving my body more. I want to have more energy and get healthier," Gloria declared.

As we discussed what a plan would look like for her, I asked, "Why is it important for you to get healthier and have more energy?"

She paused briefly and responded, "I have a beautiful family; my grandkids are so special to me."

Her face brightened as she smiled. "I want to be able to do fun activities with my grandkids, like play with them on the floor building Legos, riding bikes, and be around for them for a long time."

As we discussed what it would take to manage her stress, I asked her what she did to rest. She shared how difficult it was for her to rest. She wasn't a woman who was good at being still. Even the idea made her feel guilty. But she was willing to try. So we brainstormed a few ways she could begin to practice resting, and that's where she started, taking time to enjoy five or ten minutes doing nothing but deep breathing exercises.

She acknowledged that it wouldn't be easy but was ready to try. I encouraged her to take this on as her "new adventure" for the week, exploring where she could sprinkle in a few minutes of rest in her day. I reminded her to ask herself one simple question when it felt difficult, "How does it get to be easy?"

For Gloria, it was simple. "I will sit outside and enjoy nature in the evening after dinner."

And she did. That's where change started for Gloria.

The next step was creating a list of ideas on how to sprinkle self-care minutes into her day. She admitted teaching first graders might make this problematic. But, as we brainstormed where she could implement a few strategies in her day, she realized she was already incorporating little rest breaks in her class time, like deep breathing, stretching, and closing their eyes quietly for a few minutes to help them reset between activities. Her students were doing it, but she wasn't.

So instead of rushing to get everything together for the next activity while her students closed their eyes, she would practice a few minutes of rest and do the same as her students. After taking these few minutes to reset and focus, she reported feeling calmer. She noticed the difference in the kids' behavior as they appeared much more focused on their work after taking these short breaks throughout their day.

One of Gloria's biggest goals was to focus on learning the habit of nourishing herself consistently with good meals. Rather than skipping meals or throwing food together at the last minute, she wanted to develop a plan to help her and her husband eat healthier. Her husband had already suffered one heart attack, and her medical provider threatened to put Gloria on medication if she didn't improve her lab numbers. Gloria didn't want to go on medication. This was another strong piece of her why. She knew having a solid meal plan could benefit her and her husband, especially their health.

Her biggest roadblock was the one thing we all struggle with the most: "When do I have time to make a plan and implement it?"

So, we worked on creating intentional time in her schedule for making her meal plan. What I know to be true is that if something is a priority and we have a good reason for doing it, we will make the time for it.

"What will having a plan for your meals do for you?" I asked.

Gloria replied, "Well, by having our meals planned, I won't constantly wonder what I'm making for dinner, and that will take a load off my mind. I'll also know we'll eat healthy food because I'll be more intentional about making good choices."

"Why is that important to you, and what will it do for you in the long run?" I asked, seeing her face begin to light up across the Zoom call.

"I know if we eat better, I will have more energy. I may not have to go on medication, either. In the long run, we have a better chance of living longer and being around for our grandkids. That would make me so happy," she replied.

I knew if Gloria could see that having a plan for her meals meant she would get more time and have more energy, she would believe in it.

The decline of regular family meals is a concerning factor in the current health crisis in our country. Shockingly, only 30 percent of people still partake in family meals. Restoring this tradition could change the health of an entire nation. Reconnecting with our loved ones over shared meals serves as a protective shield for our overall well-being.

Harvard's research underscores the substantial health advantages of families consistently eating together. The study shared that children who had consistent family meals increased their intake of vital nutrients, guarding them against chronic diseases and consuming fewer unhealthy, ultra-processed foods. Children who share family meals at least three times a week demonstrate lower instances of obesity and eating disorders.[13] Other research among office workers underscores the transformative impact of regular family dinners. These gatherings contribute to elevated work morale, reduced stress, and heightened work performance.

This holds enormous significance because stress remains a prominent catalyst for chronic diseases. Reinstating the tradition of family meals is a preventative step in safeguarding our health and well-being in a world marked by disconnection and fast-paced living.

How often do you finish your workday and then ask, "What will we have for dinner?" It's funny because making dinner is something we do every day but not having a plan can make it super stressful. I've been there many times. I was the one mainly responsible for cooking in my family, and even though we loved having meals together, it often felt like a big chore. I may not be a master chef, but I was lucky to have learned the basics through programs like 4-H and home economics and had my mom, dad, and grandmothers teach me some valuable cooking skills. But one common issue I hear often among families is their need for more cooking knowledge. Many end up relying on frozen or packaged meals filled with preservatives and chemicals or eating out, which strains budgets even more and affects long-term health.

As I think back to when my kids were in middle school, they would come home saying how their friends were eager to trade Lunchables® for their home-cooked meals. I didn't think much of it at the time. But then this issue caught my attention when Kyle and Kaitlyn went to college, and both had similar experiences. They taught roommates and some of their friends basic cooking skills, like boiling water for pasta or mixing up a batch of pancakes.

The societal habit of resorting to fast food, doing everything for our kids, and prioritizing convenience over nutrition hinders them from learning essential skills and leaves them at risk for shorter life expectancies. We often resort to the convenience of fast food and processed meals, sacrificing our health for quick fixes loaded with excessive sugar, unhealthy fats, and artificial ingredients. This disconnects us from the joy and benefits of preparing, savoring, and sharing nourishing food with our families, and our bodies pay the price.

In the past, mothers, grandmothers, other family members, and home economics classes were the custodians of culinary knowledge, passing down their expertise with love and patience. They taught us the art of cooking, emphasizing the value of nourishing our bodies and nurturing our souls with good food.

Yet, in today's fast-paced reality, the demands placed on parents, particularly women, have become overwhelming because of that Messy Web. We are looking for ways to cook faster, sometimes shoving our kids out of the kitchen while trying to provide a meal for ourselves and our families.

This is where having a plan and incorporating some time to prepare healthy meals can benefit everyone.

It may feel like more work, but the payoff of having a plan is that it reduces decision fatigue, saves time and money, and provides wholesome meals for ourselves and our families. An incredible opportunity awaits us in the kitchen—to share responsibilities, teach valuable skills, and delegate tasks among family members, including our spouses and children. By involving everyone in the cooking process, we not only pass on the joy of preparing nourishing meals but also empower them with essential life skills. Together, we can create a collaborative environment where everyone has a role. This lightens our burdens and fosters a sense of responsibility and confidence in our loved ones. Through this culinary journey, we can forge stronger family bonds and embrace a healthier, more balanced lifestyle. When we eat healthier, we all win!

Gloria's journey towards healthier eating continued with a decisive change in her routine—meal planning and prepping. She started by carving out a small window of time on her weekend to plan her meals for the upcoming week. She created a meal plan that included a variety of quality foods that she enjoyed, like fresh vegetables and fruits. She ordered groceries at a local store with a pick-up option to make the process even more convenient. Her supportive husband even stepped in to help with grocery pick-up, lightening her workload and sharing the responsibilities.

Gloria and her husband became a team and accountability partners for each other, sharing a common goal. They cooked a few meals on the weekend together to provide lunches or leftovers during the week. Her husband took the lead in cooking at least one evening during the week. They found their way by experimenting, realizing the benefits of having meals together, and sharing their responsibilities, which allowed their relationship to grow.

In our coaching session, Gloria shared, "My husband and I have become focused on eating better by having a meal plan. Incorporating this with my rest plan has been life-changing. I feel so much better and got my recent blood work results. It showed my blood sugar and hormones are going in the right direction and getting close to normal limits. I've lost a few pounds and don't have to go on medication!"

Gloria's journey didn't stop there. With our work together, she understood that lasting change is best achieved one step at a time. Having a consistent meal plan in place, she noticed the difference in her energy level, allowing her to be more intentional about focusing next on foods that were better options, getting more nutrients in her meals by reading labels, and looking for foods that were less processed. She saved her weekly meal plan for a month to recycle so that she had at least four weeks of meal planning ready. This approach made it easier to integrate planning and prepping into her lifestyle. She continued to drop weight and her doctor was happy with her amazing progress.

Here are five key strategies that were central to Gloria's journey. This is your chance to try these tips so that you can focus on the planning of consistent, nutritionally sound meals throughout your week. Try these strategies to help make the transition towards healthier eating easier and more sustainable for you and your family.

1. Check Your Mindset

Now, pause and examine your perspective on meal planning and preparation. What's your mindset when it comes to this task? If you find it daunting or challenging, understand the way you are thinking about it can influence your reality. The great news is that you hold the power to change your perspective. Once you realize the numerous benefits that meal planning can bring into your life, you'll come to value the long-term advantages it offers for your health and overall well-being.

2. Know Your "Why"

Let's dive deeper into your why. Why is meal planning important to you? What do you hope to achieve by having a structured meal plan? Your reasons serve as your motivation. They can be powerful drivers of positive change in your life. They were for

Gloria. Take a moment to reflect on your own unique "why", as it will guide you to realize the benefits it has for you.

3. Make the Time

To succeed at this, it's crucial to prioritize meal planning just as you would a doctor's appointment or a work meeting. Treat it as an essential commitment in your schedule and establish clear boundaries as we discussed in chapter 5. Utilize the strategies we covered to help you stay on track.

Another key to success is finding an organizational system that suits your style. Whether it's a meal planning app, a physical planner, or a simple notepad, choose a method that aligns with your preferences and stick with it. For example, buy prechopped vegetables to help save you time. Another example is taking a few minutes to clean your produce right after your shop. Many small efforts like these can save you precious time during the week. Remember, the goal is to discover what works best for you and your unique schedule.

4. Quick and Easy for Busy Nights

Let's consider your family's schedule when it comes to meal planning. If you're well aware of those evenings when everyone's heading in different directions, having a meal plan can be a true lifesaver in more ways than one. Frequent dining out can quickly deplete your finances, and meal planning offers the advantage of controlling your expenses. By purchasing groceries in advance and sidestepping expensive last-minute dining choices, you'll have fewer financial worries during those hectic evenings.

For added convenience, consider investing in kitchen tools like a slow cooker, air fryer, or Instant Pot®. These appliances are excellent for preparing meals quickly or in advance. A slow cooker or crockpot allows you to assemble your ingredients in the morning, set the timer, and return home to a piping hot, homemade meal.

On less busy days, prepare extra portions, and you'll have a delightful meal ready to reheat when things get hectic. Soups, in particular, are versatile and can be prepared in large batches. They're not only hearty and nutritious but also ideal for reheating.

5. Let It Be Fun and Involve Others

Involve your family members in the meal planning process. This is a wonderful chance to share the workload and impart valuable cooking skills. It can also become a fun family bonding experience.

To add some fun to your meal planning, consider incorporating theme nights. Think "Meatless Mondays," "Taco Tuesdays," or "Italian Thursdays." Themes inject excitement into your meal planning and help you establish a well-structured plan.

For added convenience, explore online or local meal planning services. These services can simplify the process by providing recipes, shopping lists, and ready-made healthy meals, making your meal planning journey smoother and more enjoyable.

Now It's Your Turn

What is your current meal planning strategy?
How does or would meal planning benefit you?
What are your biggest meal planning challenges?
What can you do to overcome them?

Eating What Is Right for You

Jessica felt drained and fatigued. Every day was a struggle. She spent more and more time confined to her home. It wasn't by choice but by necessity. Her energy levels had plummeted, leaving her with little strength to do much else. Going out to socialize or be in public settings filled her with anxiety about having an "accident" caused by the constant flare-ups of her irritable bowel syndrome (IBS). This made leaving the house a daunting activity.

The stress in Jessica's life had reached an all-time high. Her adult daughter, who had three kids, had just been through a difficult separation from her husband. Jessica and her husband were trying to help their daughter navigate a new life as a single mom. They were suddenly thrown into a co-parenting situation and felt they had no choice but to help her with her life circumstances, especially financially. While Jessica couldn't ignore the mounting responsibilities, she felt the world's weight on her shoulders.

With her husband often away for work during the week, Jessica relied on convenience foods—take-out meals, processed snacks, sugary treats, and sometimes even skipping meals altogether. These choices were wreaking havoc on her body, exacerbating her IBS symptoms. Nausea, diarrhea, and the constant fear of not making it to the bathroom in time had become her daily vicious cycle. The unpredictability of her condition was a constant source of anxiety.

It was at this challenging juncture that she decided to seek help. Jessica came to me for life coaching, but what it turned into was so much more.

On our first Zoom call, I asked her, "What feels like your biggest challenge right now?"

With a tired look in her eyes, she responded, "I just don't know where to start. I feel like my life is so out of control."

As we talked more, I asked her, "What do you think would help you feel more in control of your life?"

She replied, "I know I need to learn how to eat healthier, which would probably help me feel better. But I think if I figure out how to get control of my time first, I will feel less overwhelmed. Finding time to focus on taking care of me feels impossible right now."

I could hear that Jessica wanted to find some way to balance helping her take care of herself and being able to take care of her daughter and grandkids as well. We began by addressing the stress in Jessica's life and what parts of her life she could control. Recognizing Jessica had a lot of demands in her life, we started with small, manageable steps. Together, we discovered the first step was to reclaim her time. We looked at prioritizing her calendar, and she clarified her priorities through the *Priority Power-Up Practice* we covered in chapter 5. We also had to work on her mindset about allowing time to care for herself—something we will cover in the next chapter.

Next, she decided the first fifteen minutes of her morning would start with quiet morning prayer. She had had this practice a few years earlier and admitted she missed it. This simple practice allowed Jessica to center herself and set a positive tone for the day. She felt more focused and in control of her emotions on the days when she had this practice versus the days she didn't.

Each week, Jessica began to build small blocks of time in her day to add intentional rest. After those habits were locked in place, she was ready to focus on her eating habits. She understood and recognized the importance of a nourishing breakfast and decided to try a protein-filled smoothie with green veggies and fruit. This provided essential nutrients and stabilized her blood sugar levels, curbing her snacking.

However, the real game-changer was when Jessica got curious about her sugar cravings. She learned the detrimental effects of excessive sugar consumption, which was present in almost every processed food she had been consuming. She decided to eliminate as much of the processed foods high in sugar from her daily menu.

She approached this with curiosity and started looking at the labels of foods and recognizing ingredients that were triggering her digestive issues. She focused on incorporating quality natural foods into her diet and balancing her plate to her body's needs.

The transformation was astonishing. Within a few weeks, Jessica significantly increased her energy levels. Her stomach troubles and belly bloat subsided, and the fear of IBS-related accidents became less frequent. Jessica realized that slowing down, prioritizing nourishing foods, and replacing processed foods with more nutritious, nutrient-dense options was the combination that worked best for her.

On our coaching call, Jessica was excited to share her celebrations. I couldn't help but notice the difference in Jessica's eyes on this call versus our first call. She looked more rested and seemed much more excited about what she was doing.

Jessica shared, "I've learned valuable lessons about myself and that my choices make a big difference in how I feel and show up each day. Making space on my calendar made time for me, something I needed to allow myself to do."

"That's great you learned that about yourself. I can see the difference in your energy on our call today. Are there any other lessons you've learned?" I asked, feeling excited to hear more.

"I learned how addicted I was to sugar and how much it was slowing me down. I can't believe it was in almost everything I was eating, and by removing processed foods from my daily plate and making healthier choices, I am amazed at how much better I feel," Jessica declared.

This was life-changing for Jessica. It wasn't just about *what* she ate but about understanding *how* her choices impacted her body and how it made her feel emotionally too. Jessica had taken charge of her choices and was now living a life full of energy, optimism, and freedom from the chains of IBS.

In the race for convenience, it's easy to overlook the incredible benefits that lie within the food we consume daily. But here's a secret: our foods are the key to unlocking the remarkable potential of our bodies. Natural, whole foods are nature's medicine, offering a natural way to nourish, heal, and thrive. Imagine indulging in the extraordinary power of pure ingredients straight from nature's pantry. That's what whole foods are. Visualize savoring the crispness of a garden-fresh salad, relishing the sweetness of a ripe summer peach, and basking in the comforting warmth of a hearty homemade soup. Whole foods can become the cornerstone of your meals, providing a splendid array of colors, textures, and flavors.

When we consume processed foods loaded with refined sugars, unhealthy fats, and artificial additives, we unwittingly fuel the fire of inflammation, wreaking havoc on our body's delicate balance, especially in our gut microbiome. Chronic inflammation, triggered by these dietary choices, can lead to long-term health issues and leave us feeling less than our best.

Dr. Mark Hyman, M.D., the host of the podcast, *The Doctor's Farmacy*, emphasizes the profound impact of our diets on chronic diseases and the healing power of food. He states:

"Our diets are the main driver of the chronic disease epidemic we are experiencing today. But food is also the most powerful medicine available to heal chronic diseases. The food we eat literally serves as information, instructions, or code that controls almost every function of the body—including our hormones, appetite, brain chemistry, immune system, gene expression, and even the microbiome. Food is real medicine, and it's actually more effective—most of the time—than pharmacology for chronic disease. You can do things with food that you can't do with most drugs."[14]

This concept has caught the attention of medical education programs, which are finally beginning to incorporate programs like lifestyle and culinary medicine as part of their curriculum. Still, much work is needed in our medical care system and our mindset on how we view food as part of our solution. This is why it's even more important to take charge of our choices and focus on what we each need to thrive and feel our best.

Balancing your plate is about more than adhering to rigid dietary rules. It's about recognizing and responding to what your unique body requires. There is no one-size-fits-all approach here; it's about understanding that we all have different needs. It's all about fine-tuning the food on your plate to create a sense of satisfaction and fullness that carries you seamlessly from one meal to the next.

Take, for example, a client who found themselves ravenous at 10:00 a.m., well before lunchtime. Through awareness and experimentation, she could tailor her breakfast to stop those mid-morning hunger pangs by experimenting with different combinations of protein, healthy fats, low-impact carbohydrates, fruits, and vegetables. It's all about balance, but more importantly, finding what works for your unique body.

When coaching clients who are finding it challenging to transition to healthier foods, meeting them where they're at is important. It's essential to understand their unique situations and concerns. Many are apprehensive about completely overhauling their eating habits, so I often ask them to reflect on their fondest healthy food memories. This typically involves asking (through stories), about the meals they cherished, often drawing from childhood experiences.

For example, one client fondly recalled her summer days picking strawberries and blueberries with her mom and how refreshing those berries were. Another client remembered cooking a yummy vegetable soup with their grandmother. This exercise helps in two ways. First, it reignites a positive and emotional connection with food, and second, it opens the door to the idea that healthy foods can be enjoyable and nourishing.

The next step revolves around experimentation. Instead of pushing individuals to make drastic changes, we explore how we can gradually infuse more color and nutritional value into their food choices. We don't immediately replace all white rice and pasta with brown rice or quinoa; instead, we discuss the best options they are willing to try. The focus is creating a sustainable and enjoyable transition, one step at a time.

A food diary is another valuable tool for enhancing your relationship with nutrition and making informed choices by encouraging mindfulness. By jotting down everything you eat, you become more aware and identify patterns in your eating habits. For instance, you might notice tendencies to overeat during specific times of the day or when experiencing stress.

Keeping a food diary also creates a sense of accountability. Knowing that each food choice will be documented can motivate you to make healthier choices. It aids in understanding appropriate portion sizes, making it easier to recognize when you're consistently overeating or undereating. A food diary can highlight emotional eating triggers, helping you differentiate between eating in response to hunger or other emotions like stress or boredom. You can identify foods that make you feel your best and those that don't. It can also be a powerful tool for setting and achieving specific dietary goals. You can monitor your progress toward increasing vegetable consumption, reducing added sugars, or staying hydrated.

Exploring nourishing and healthy food options isn't about deprivation or strict rules. It's about embracing a mindset of abundance and curiosity, something we will cover in the next chapter. You're laying the foundation for a healthier life by making mindful choices and prioritizing nourishment. This approach builds a foundation for long-lasting lifestyle changes and food choices that align with their goals and aspirations.

My role as a health and wellness coach doesn't involve prescribing, treating, or providing specific diets. Instead, I help clients stay accountable to the dietary plan they have collaborated on with their medical providers. Dietary recommendations, especially for specific health conditions, should always be discussed with a medical professional or a registered dietitian who can offer personalized advice and prescribe appropriate diets.

What I provide is helping you brainstorm options, asking questions to explore your opportunities to change through curiosity, and empowering you with knowledge and ideas for a healthier lifestyle. While the following suggestions can serve as a starting point, they are by no means an exhaustive list.

For more evidence based information about food and nutrition choices, visit the US Department of Health and Human Services, Office of Disease Prevention and Health Promotion at https://health.gov. Working collaboratively with healthcare professionals is crucial to effectively address your unique health needs.

Jessica's story is an inspiring example of taking control of one's health, leading to a life characterized by vitality, positivity, and freedom from the constraints of IBS. So, what's best for you?

Here are some things to consider when creating your balanced, healthy plate.

Non-Starchy Vegetables and Fruits

Non-starchy vegetables and fruits provide a spectrum of essential nutrients, antioxidants, and dietary fiber that support overall health, weight management, and disease prevention. Their low-calorie content and high nutritional value make them valuable to any balanced and nourishing diet. From leafy greens like spinach and kale to vibrant berries, every plant-based food carries its health benefits.

Maximize your nutritional diversity by including colorful, non-starchy vegetables and fruits in your meals by considering things like brussels sprouts, broccoli, spinach, kale, cauliflower, squash, zucchini, carrots, cabbage, sauerkraut, and cucumbers. Each color represents a unique set of vitamins, minerals, and antioxidants that contribute to your nutritionally balanced plate.

Slow-Impact Carbohydrates

The gradual energy release from slow-impact carbohydrates helps stabilize blood sugar levels, providing long-lasting energy and promoting feelings of fullness. Including these foods in your meals can help you maintain consistent energy levels, control your appetite, and support your overall health.

Many options include quinoa, wild rice, and oats, which provide a wealth of fiber, vitamins, and minerals. Lentils, butternut squash, raspberries, blueberries, green apples, acorn squash, sweet potatoes, and oatmeal make a satisfying meal foundation. Enjoy them in various forms, from warm breakfast porridges to hearty grain bowls and side dishes. Exploring whole grain options adds nutritional value and exciting textures and flavors to your plate.

High-Quality Protein Sources

High-quality proteins are a fundamental part of a balanced diet, as they supply our bodies with vital amino acids necessary for tissue repair, hormone production, immune system support, and muscle development. These proteins can be sourced from various options, including wild-caught fish, salmon, grass-fed beef, pastured eggs, and plant-based alternatives like chickpeas, lentils, and beans.

These options offer not only protein but also fiber and essential nutrients, making them suitable for a range of dishes, from soups to salads. You can even incorporate tofu or tempeh into your cooking to diversify your protein-rich, nutritious, and versatile meal choices.

Healthy Fats

Healthy fats are crucial for brain function and hormone production. Avocados, walnuts, flax seeds, chia seeds, grass-fed ghee, coconut, and olive oil are all excellent sources of heart-healthy fats that can be incorporated into your meals and snacks. They provide satiety, enhance the absorption of fat-soluble vitamins, and contribute to a well-rounded and nourishing diet.

Hydration

Adequate hydration plays a crucial role in the overall function of our bodies, including digestion, nutrient absorption, circulation, temperature regulation, and waste elimination. It also helps maintain the balance of bodily fluids, promotes healthy skin, boosts energy levels, reduces sugar cravings, and supports cognitive function. It even has the potential to enhance our mood and reduce fatigue.

While water is the ultimate hydrator, other delicious and nutritious beverages can contribute to our hydration goals. Herbal teas, infused water with fruits or herbs, coconut water, and natural fruit juices can add variety and flavor to our hydration routine. It's important to be mindful of added sugars and artificial additives in certain beverages, so reading labels and opting for natural, low-sugar options is recommended.

Consult with your medical provider to discuss your specific hydration needs and ensure you consume appropriate water if you have any health concerns. Remember, staying hydrated is not only crucial during physical exertion or hot weather; it's a daily commitment to help us function properly.

A balanced plate is a unique journey for each individual, and prioritizing nourishing foods while swapping processed options for nutrient-dense choices can lead to transformative results. Jessica's experience illustrates the life-changing potential of these choices. It goes beyond the mere act of eating; it's about comprehending how our dietary decisions affect our overall well-being.

Now It's Your Turn

How do your current eating habits support your balanced plate?
Do you notice certain foods that give you energy or take energy away?
What are the biggest challenges when creating your balanced plate?
What can you do to overcome them?

Moving Your Body

Clients often ask, "What's the best type of exercise I should be doing?"

It's a common question, and my answer is straightforward: "The best exercise is the one you'll do. What do you enjoy when it comes to moving your body?"

It might seem like a different approach to fitness, but it's the route to discovering what you genuinely enjoy instead of forcing yourself into a grueling workout you despise. The gym membership won't do you much good if you don't enjoy going to the gym, or you won't use that elliptical in your bedroom if it has become the display of your clothes from the week. So, how about flipping the script on how you think about exercising and trying simple, fun ways to move your body throughout your day instead?

As a Nationally Board Certified Health and Wellness Coach, I specialize in asking the right questions to help you find the right answer rather than giving you a prescription. The answers lie within you, and my role is to guide you in finding what works best for your unique situation and needs. It's about empowering clients to take control of their well-being and make lasting, positive changes.

This approach opens up a great discussion where we explore what works best for each individual. It's not about following the latest fitness trends or adhering to a specific regimen; it's about discovering what forms of movement bring joy and satisfaction to your unique body. By exploring preferences and finding activities you genuinely love, you can create a personalized and sustainable movement approach to help your body thrive and enjoy it.

Exploring and experimenting with different types of movement help us discover what makes our body feel our best. Whether it's the graceful flow of yoga, the rhythmic beat of a dance class, the grounding power of strength training, or the exhilarating rush of outdoor activities, the key is finding what brings us alive and ignites our passion for movement.

Movement is not merely a chore to check off a list. Integrating movement into our daily routines is key to maintaining our energy throughout the day. This isn't about adhering to strict schedules or punishing ourselves with intense workouts. Instead, it's about embracing the inherent beauty of movement and infusing our lives with activities that have us moving without any stressful objective. This can be as simple as opting for the stairs instead of the elevator, taking a stroll outside enjoying nature, or even spontaneously breaking into a dance party in the comfort of our living room. It's all movement, and every step makes a difference.

I particularly love the concept I call "snack-size" movement. It encourages us to seize those brief ten-minute breaks or slivers of time and transform them into rejuvenating moments of physical activity. Whether taking a few laps around the office building or dancing into a refreshed state of mind, these small bursts of movement can profoundly elevate mood, improve energy levels, and add to the numerous benefits for our bodies.

Remember that movement is not a burden but a gift—a testament to the strength and resilience that reside within us. As my friend Amy Peele, author, yoga instructor, and retired nurse, beautifully puts it, "Motion is lotion!" This simple phrase reminds us to keep our bodies fluid and spirits flowing to feel our best.

As the sun set on a beautiful walk I shared with a friend one evening, she said, "I never regret moving my body; I only regret it when I don't."

These words encapsulate the profound truth that lies at the core of our being. Each step, each motion, affirms our commitment to embrace life's richness and savor the blessings of our body's capability.

> ### *Now It's Your Turn*
>
> *What are the ways you enjoy moving your body?*
> *How can you incorporate "snack-size" movement into your day?*
> *What would help you get started or be consistent in moving your body?*

Embracing the Healing Power of Sleep

In my late twenties, I worked as a respiratory therapist in a busy trauma hospital.

Working the night shift meant my sleep schedule was far from regular. I found myself navigating through the challenges of a full-time position with twelve-hour night shifts, all while enduring a forty-five-minute commute each way. Exhausted and in need of comfort, I developed a ritual of stopping at McDonald's on my way home to savor a bacon, egg, and cheese biscuit and orange juice, providing solace during those lonely drives to keep me awake.

Those days and nights were rough. My sleep patterns became erratic, leaving me with just a few hours here and there. I recall the sheer relief of crawling into bed after a hot shower, the comforting embrace of warmth and clean sheets. As soon as my head hit the pillow, I would drift off into a much-needed slumber. However, a few hours later, the sunlight would pierce through the curtains and wake me up. Frustrated, I'd toss a pillow over my head, desperately attempting to block out the light and return to sleep, only to find myself wide awake despite feeling exhausted.

Living on autopilot became the norm for me. I was merely "functioning" daily, going through the motions.

Then one day, as I opened our electric bill statement, I discovered we had an $800 credit. Confusion turned into delight as I marveled at this unexpected gift. Then the delight turned into horror. I couldn't believe it. I had inadvertently written a check for the entire balance of our checking account to the electric company!

After a frantic call to the service department, the polite lady kindly thanked me for the advance payment of our electric bill and declared a refund wasn't possible. Frustrated and foggy-eyed, this wake-up call made me realize that sleep is far more than just a luxury; it is a vital resource that profoundly affects how we function. It became clear that I needed to prioritize and protect my sleep as one of my most valuable assets.

You're not alone if you struggle with a lack of sleep or poor sleep quality. According to the Centers for Disease Control and Prevention (CDC), most adults require at least seven hours of sleep for optimal health. Shockingly, a staggering one-third of adults in the United States have struggled to get sufficient sleep.[15]

Quality sleep is essential for physical health, mental clarity, emotional balance, and a healthy immune system. Without sufficient and restorative sleep, our bodies become more vulnerable to different health issues, such as chronic diseases, obesity, mood disorders, and cognitive decline.

If you are working to improve sleep, cracking your code for a good night's sleep is like being a sleep detective. It's all about gathering clues, conducting experiments, and unlocking the secrets to help listen to what your body needs. Now, more than ever, it's time to unravel the mystery of rejuvenating sleep and supercharging it. There are many puzzle pieces—find the ones that help you!

Here are six essential components to set yourself up for quality sleep.

Set up a Comfortable Sleep Environment

When it comes to your sleep haven, you want it to be calm, dark, and serene. Don't hesitate to use earplugs, eye masks, or a white noise machine to avoid disruptions. And let's talk decor; think soft, calming colors, plush bedding, and gentle lighting for those cozy vibes. Consider adding natural elements, like plants. Declutter your sleep zone; a tidy room means a tranquil mind. Getting rid of that unnecessary stuff and keeping things organized can help bring peace and promote deep sleep.

Create a Calming Routine with Consistency

Our bodies love routines. You might remember having a bedtime routine as a kid. But as adults, we often toss those routines aside. Yet, by creating a consistent sleep schedule where you go to bed and wake up at the same time every day (yes, even on weekends), you can help your body regulate its internal clock and boost your sleep quality. Engaging in calming activities like reading, enjoying a warm bath, or trying gentle stretches and deep breathing exercises can signal to your body that it's time to relax and get ready for sleep.

Limit the Screens

Consider removing electronic devices from your bedroom such as TVs, computers, or gaming consoles. These devices emit stimulating light and tempt you to engage in activities that keep your mind active instead of preparing for sleep. The blue light emitted by electronic devices like smartphones, tablets, or laptops can disrupt your sleep by suppressing the production of melatonin, a hormone that regulates sleep. Aim to avoid using these devices at least one hour before bedtime, and use blue light glasses to help prevent overexposure to blue light.

Notice How Certain Foods Affect Your Sleep

Caffeinated beverages such as soda, coffee, and tea can disrupt sleep. Similarly, drinking alcohol, though it may initially make you drowsy, can disrupt sleep cycles, leading to less restorative rest. Avoiding heavy, spicy, and large meals close to bedtime can prevent discomfort and indigestion, promoting sound sleep. Foods high in sugar and processed carbs may cause nighttime awakenings due to blood sugar fluctuations. Stay hydrated during the day, but avoid excessive fluids near bedtime to minimize nighttime awakenings. Opt for a balanced diet, including nutrient-rich foods like magnesium sources (leafy greens and nuts), to positively influence your sleep.

Get Moving, Embrace Sunlight, and Connect to the Earth

Engage in regular movement in your day. If you like to do a more intense workout, try to finish it a few hours before bedtime, as exercise can increase your alertness and make it harder to fall asleep. Adequate exposure to natural sunlight is crucial in regulating our body's circadian rhythm. Exposure to morning sunlight can promote alertness during the day and enhance the quality of nighttime sleep by signaling to the body that it's time to rest.

Grounding, also known as earthing, involves making direct contact with the Earth's surface, such as walking barefoot on grass, putting your hands in your flowerbeds, or swimming in a pool or ocean. Ever wonder why you sleep better after a day at the beach? Studies suggest that grounding can help reduce stress and inflammation, improving sleep quality. The Earth's surface carries a negative electrical charge and, when we connect with it, it may help neutralize free radicals and promote a state of relaxation conducive to better sleep. So charge up!

Manage Your Stress and Release Your Worries

What if you tried all of these suggestions and it's still difficult to sleep? This is where the role of our nervous system comes into play. During stressful times, like the height of the pandemic, our sympathetic nervous system, often called the "fight or flight" response, can go into overdrive. This heightened alertness, with worries and anxieties about the world, can seep into our sleep patterns.

Finding ways to calm the nervous system through relaxation techniques, mindfulness, or even seeking professional help can be incredibly beneficial for achieving restful sleep, even in the face of challenging times.

Let me tell you about Rachel. Rachel was a successful entrepreneur who struggled with her sleep. She tried to shut off her racing thoughts every night. She tried to shut off her racing thoughts every night, but she was often waking up exhausted. Rachel tried everything she could think of—pills, meditation, and exercise routine —but nothing seems to work.

When I asked Rachel to walk me through a day in her life, I could quickly hear that her schedule was hectic and overscheduled with little downtime. The pace at which she went through her day was exhausting. She raced from dropping the kids off at school, back home to begin her work day in her remote job, sitting at her desk most of the day with tight deadlines on projects, and Zoom conferences with her support staff. After work, she immediately began her second shift of juggling her entire family's schedule, from the football games to dance practices to evening business events, not to mention making dinner and managing her home.

Early in our coaching sessions, she cleared and delegated things from her hefty responsibilities at work and home. She established a good plan for healthy meals for her family, implementing a combination of weekend meal prep and a local affordable meal service. She noticed how much lighter she felt working on these few things.

But her mind was still having a hard time shutting off at night. As she told me more about her evening routine, she admitted she didn't allow herself much time to slow down. She wanted to focus on ways to get better sleep. As we brainstormed, I saw her excitement about trying a few strategies.

One of those strategies was to get more movement and outside time during her day by infusing a short burst of fresh air, activity, and sunshine. She started seeing small pockets of time to take a ten-minute walk outside or have lunch in the sun when the weather permitted. She spent most of her day inside at her desk, so it was a welcome way to move her body and get some fresh air and sunshine. This was a way for Rachel to reset, feeling more focused and reenergized when she returned to work.

She also implemented a strategy called the *Power Down Hour*. This allowed Rachel to create a bedtime routine that started at 9:00 p.m. to shut off her electric devices, and her body took the cue that it was time to slow down. She decided to take thirty minutes to tidy up last-minute things for the kids, and then she would start at 9:30 p.m. with a thirty-minute bath, followed by fifteen minutes to do the *Brain Dump Practice* to help her with the thoughts racing through her mind before bed. This simple act helped Rachel clear her mind of all the worries and concerns keeping her up at night.

On her midweek check-in, she said, "I did my Power Down Hour this last week with some journaling time and noticed I feel less overwhelmed and more focused these last few days. I slept so much better."

Seeing the positive effects of this practice, we also focused on beliefs about unbusying the mind. Rachel had always believed she needed to be constantly busy to succeed, something we will dive into in the next chapter. However, with weekly accountability and support, Rachel began to see that taking time to slow down and rest was just as important as working hard.

Rachel discovered the intricate connections between her sleep, diet, and physical activity, decluttering her schedule, managing expectations, and nurturing her thoughts. It became evident that these factors significantly influence the quality of sleep, and in turn, rest has a profound impact on all aspects of her life.

Rachel's story is a testament to the power of prioritizing sleep. As she experimented with making small changes one week at a time, the positive change had a cascading effect on her daily life. Waking up feeling refreshed and energized enhanced her focus and motivated her throughout the day. Ultimately, Rachel's journey highlighted a crucial lesson—caring for her mind was just as vital as caring for her body. Through our collaborative efforts, she was able to revamp her sleep habits and discover a new approach to relaxation, ensuring that she could easily drift off into a restful sleep.

> ### *Now It's Your Turn*
>
> *How many hours of sleep do you typically aim for each night?*
> *How do you feel when you get a good night's sleep?*
> *What's one change you would like to try to help you sleep better?*

Putting It All Into Practice

Barbara's life had transformed into a storm of frustration and unhappiness. She had reached a breaking point, grappling with the challenge of shedding the fifteen pounds she had gained over the past year. The relentless struggle of calorie counting, persistent bloating, and stomach discomfort marred her days. But her challenges went far beyond her physical health.

As the primary caregiver for her ailing mother, she carried a tremendous burden. Despite her mom residing in an assisted living facility, Barbara managed the intricate complexity of doctor's appointments, financial responsibilities, and numerous calls to the insurance company, accountant, and financial advisor. Barbara was responsible for moving her mother across the country to live close to her despite having two other siblings who agreed she was the best choice.

With the overwhelming responsibilities, the peaceful morning routine of a long walk with her dog had become a distant memory. Her quiet morning devotional time was replaced by the urgency of other tasks. Her participation in the cherished Bible study group dwindled due to conflicting medical appointments. The crafting projects that once brought her joy now lay abandoned in a spare room, collecting dust. Her exhaustion had taken a toll on her, leading to a strained relationship with her husband. Barbara felt disconnected from herself, alone, and questioning the person she had become.

"I've abandoned my needs, and the stress and pressure from caring for my mom has put a strain on my relationship with my husband," Barbara confided, her eyes brimming with tears. "As I attended your workshop, it struck me that I haven't even considered my stress as the culprit for not losing weight."

Barbara recognized the need for change, but the path ahead seemed daunting, burdened with her juggling many responsibilities. Her previous attempts at weight loss through calorie restriction and liquid diet supplements had only left her disappointed, as the weight she shed had a habit of returning.

As we talked, Barbara expressed her frustration and confusion about where to start. The overwhelming abundance of information on diets, exercise routines, and self-care practices left her needing guidance to find the right path. She wondered if it was possible to break free from her current state and carve out a way to care for herself, all while bearing the weight of her demanding responsibilities.

Together, we explored Barbara's desires, taking a holistic look at how the various facets of her life intertwined. We started by shaping her vision with the *Wheel of Life* exercise, examining the top five areas of her life.

During our session, I asked, "What would you like your health to be like instead?"

Barbara passionately responded, "I want to feel more energized and connected to my body again. I don't recognize the woman in the mirror anymore."

With her vision established, we laid the groundwork for her plan, focused on the journey back to herself through rest, nutrition, movement, and social connections. Barbara initiated her plan with a clear vision and unwavering intentions, concentrating on one or two specific aspects each week. She took measured, manageable steps, ensuring they seamlessly integrated into her busy life.

Barbara initiated her first week by creating a morning routine tailored to her need for a fresh start to the day. A revitalizing walk outdoors with her dog became a cherished component of her morning ritual, reconnecting her with nature and reinvigorating her body and mind. This was followed by fifteen minutes of quiet reflection, reading from her devotional and prayer, and enjoying a nourishing breakfast smoothie.

These three nonnegotiables in her morning routine set the tone for her day, and she was determined to safeguard this time by avoiding early morning appointments for her mom, allowing her the space to start her day in the best possible way.

Next, she crafted a meal plan that prioritized nutritious foods. Barbara adopted a more mindful approach to her dietary choices, opting for foods that boosted her energy while eliminating those that left her feeling sluggish and bloated. Her focus centered on creating a well-rounded plate, involving thorough scrutiny of food labels and ingredient lists. She observed a reduction in her cravings, especially for sugary snacks, as her body received the vital nutrients she craved instead.

Barbara was intrigued by the positive impact of embracing more nutritious foods as she began to experience better energy levels and a reduced desire for sugary indulgences. Her curiosity about the role of added sugars in her diet grew more extensive, and she actively sought to seek out the hidden sugars lurking in her favorite foods, such as protein bars and condiments. This newfound knowledge empowered her to make informed choices aligned with her commitment to a healthier lifestyle.

As Barbara gradually established a structure in her meal planning and physical activity, we shifted our focus toward addressing her stress. She recognized the equal importance of reconnecting with her friends and engaging in activities she loved. While her mother resided in an assisted living facility, Barbara had the opportunity to care for herself.

However, during one of our coaching sessions, she revealed that her guilt prevented her from pursuing her passions. Barbara often made the forty-five minute trip to visit her mother, who had difficulty adjusting to her new surroundings. As we talked through her feelings of guilt, she had a profound realization. "My mom could live another ten years. I can't deny myself by not caring for myself or enjoying the activities I love for another ten years."

This was an ironic moment for both Barbara and me, as we had both struggled at one point to grant ourselves permission to prioritize our own needs. I shared my experience with her, and she confessed, "I thought it was just me."

I reassured her, "You are not alone. What steps can you take to grant yourself the permission you deserve?"

As Barbara opened up about her friends and the activities she cherished, she consciously decided to reignite her passion for reading, quilting, participating in Bible study sessions, and reconnecting with her quilting group. These moments of joy and fulfillment served as a source of strength for her spirit, and she knew that re-establishing her priorities and setting healthy boundaries were necessary to achieve this.

Together, we worked on eliminating the guilt and frustration stemming from the added pressure and societal expectations that weighed her down. Barbara took significant steps to release the guilt by identifying the thoughts that triggered these feelings, acknowledging her limited time, and delegating specific tasks to other family members or hiring assistance. These changes lightened her load and improved her relationship with her mother.

As Barbara wholeheartedly implemented these transformative changes, she witnessed the profound impact of self-care in action. Her exhaustion and feeling overwhelmed diminished, and her overall well-being improved significantly. She began to eat better, sleep soundly, and even shed ten pounds. Barbara emerged as a rejuvenated woman with a consistent movement routine and a noticeable change in how she fit into her clothes. By listening to her body's needs and giving herself the self-care she longed for, Barbara became the person she had always wanted to be.

Our journey through this chapter has explored learning the crucial aspects of listening to your body by managing stress, decluttering your surroundings, and creating stronger social connections, which can be some of the ways to help. We uncovered the significance of meal-prepping and balanced nutrition, embraced the pivotal role of moving your body, and learned the rejuvenating effects of sleep. There are many forms of rest, and each aspect of these areas is essential to our well-being and promotes rest.

I've shared my story, as well as the inspiring stories of my clients. Each of us found the ways to listen to our body and respond with what we needed. As we continue, remember that you now have the tools and the knowledge to listen in and give your body what you need! Keep tuning in!

Chapter 6 Key Takeaways

- Learning to listen to your body is a pathway to connect to who you are and your needs.

- Chronic low-level stress is one of the biggest causes of inflammation in your body and plays a significant role in your hormonal health.

- You have the power to help reduce your stress by implementing tools like *B.A.U.—Breathe, Ask, Unload.*

- Answer your craving for rest by exploring what the best kind of rest is for you.

- A clutter-free space helps clear your mind.

- Having a plan helps fuel yourself with consistent meals.

- A balanced plate combines healthy, nourishing foods that work best for your unique body.

- Strong social connections help you live a longer and happier life.

- Finding the way you love to move your body is more motivating and fun.

- Remember to always focus on what you can control.

- Start with small, manageable steps that fit into your daily life.

- Remember that what works great for someone might not be right for you.

- Find what works for you!

If you would like to practice applying the *It's Your Turn* strategies to your own life from this chapter, please use your cell phone camera to scan the QR code below or use the hyperlink at https://itsyourturnbook.com/resources.

itsyourturnbook.com/resources

Chapter 7

The Mindset of Saying "Yes" to Yourself

Our past is a story existing only in our minds. Look, analyze, understand, and forgive. Then, as quickly as possible, chuck it.
—Marianne Williamson

When our daughter Kaitlyn was in the fifth grade, John was deployed to Afghanistan. She was in a program called *Girls on the Run®*.[1] The girls met weekly with a coach after school to learn about health and fitness training to run a 5K race with focused lessons in personal empowerment.

At the conclusion of the season, they ran a non-competitive 5K race with a chosen partner, usually a parent or mentor. For the previous two years, John had been Kaitlyn's running partner. It was a special time for them to talk about the personal empowerment lessons while training for their race. My heart ached for both of them because this year, John wouldn't be by her side.

While I was not in the best physical shape to run a 5K, I did the next best thing—I called my younger, more fit sister and asked her if she could be Kaitlyn's partner for the race. I made sure she could make the two-hour flight work with her college schedule before I sprung the idea on Kaitlyn. I was relieved when my sister said yes. Kaitlyn was happy to have her aunt as her partner. It brought the excitement back into the event despite the empty void of where Dad would typically be.

I shared our plan with John on a video call that week. I saw his facial expression change. The sting of heartbreak was visible, and the sadness on his face revealed what he wasn't saying out loud. Military families struggle with missing shared moments like these. The more prominent events, like holidays, birthdays, or special occasions, are expected to be challenging. However, a different kind of grief hits when these small, memorable moments are missed. We often fail to appreciate how impactful these tiny slivers of time are until we are experiencing them.

Suddenly, John's face brightened. "What if I could participate in a different way?"

I stopped folding laundry to give him my full attention. "What do you mean?"

He started to propose a plan. My excitement grew as I visualized the plan coming together. But would it work?

On race day, John's video call came through on my phone. I picked up and brought the phone to Kaitlyn and my sister, who were pinning race tags on their shirts. As we greeted him on the screen, we saw that he was ready to run on a treadmill at the gym on Camp Leatherneck in Afghanistan. He shared a special surprise as he spanned down to the t-shirt he had specially made for the event that read, "Girls on the Run Forward Camp Leatherneck Afghanistan."

Kaitlyn smiled and was anxious to get the 5K started. My heart melted as I held back the tears.

It was a drizzly, cool morning as my sister ran beside Kaitlyn while her dad ran on a treadmill thousands of miles away, connected via FaceTime in a sleeve on my sister's arm. We prayed the Internet connection would cooperate so they could share their race. In 2013, FaceTime and Wi-Fi were less advanced and reliable than they are today.

Despite all the "what-ifs," we believed it would work, and it did! Kaitlyn saw her dad, and John saw her every step of the race. Feeling the surge of emotions as they crossed the finish line together, we all celebrated. They completed the race. As her coach and the other girls gathered at the finish line, they were amazed to see the unique idea that was made a reality. As we drove home from the event, Kaitlyn's words eased the sting of her dad's deployment, "That was awesome, Mom! It was like Dad was here in person, running right with me." I couldn't help but shed a few tears.

That experience taught me that we *get to* decide how we let our circumstances dictate our thoughts, feelings, and actions. In this case, John's optimism and creative ideas led to our results. It is an incredible memory of triumph in the face of a challenge. At the time, I only saw three possibilities: I could run the race with Kaitlyn, I could get someone else to run for me, or Kaitlyn didn't get to participate. None of the options involved my husband. I was too tired to see another way.

It's easy not to see other possibilities or be creative when we feel depleted, as we're running so fast through our everyday lives. Sometimes, we need help from others to see our blind spots. I was a busy mom of two kids involved in after-school activities, working a full-time job, and taking online classes to complete my bachelor's degree while my husband was deployed. Living day to day, I felt a constant sense of depletion and was in a fog, unable to see or think anything differently than, "These are the cards I'm dealt. This is the way it is. Press on!"

How I lived, running myself ragged, not asking for help, and thinking I had to do it all, drove my chaos and choices. Despite my efforts to stay positive, I struggled to see beyond my challenges. No amount of affirmations was going to will my way out of what I was experiencing.

At times, all I could see were problems, not opportunities. I realize now that untangling the complex network of thought patterns works in both directions—cleaning up the body also cleans up the mind, and vice versa. It's evident that merely thinking positively isn't enough. Real change requires consistent effort in our mindset, a continuous exercise of our mental muscles—something we must work on daily.

Welcome to the chapter that explores the incredible power of your mind. We will explore how our thoughts, beliefs, and mindset shape our lives and influence our personal growth. Every thought creates a ripple effect, shaping our feelings and determining our actions. For Kaitlyn and John, crossing that finish line in the race wasn't just a physical win but a win with our mindset. By becoming aware of the interplay of how our thoughts, feelings, and actions work, we can consciously reframe our thoughts and cultivate a positive mindset that empowers us. It's about rewiring our thinking patterns where we tend to have a negative bias and replacing those self-limiting beliefs with empowering ones that propel us forward.

In chapter 5, we touched on creating awareness of our self-limiting beliefs. Now, let's look at how reframing these beliefs can foster a mindset that helps us reach our goals. We will explore empowering perspectives and practical strategies to help build a positive way of thinking that involves taking care of yourself and embracing self-love, confidence in your abilities, and celebrating your wins. Get ready to claim your worth and uncover the possibilities for your abundance!

Embracing a mindset focused on what's possible allows you to see opportunities rather than obstacles. Navigating the complexities of the Messy Web and overcoming self-limiting beliefs requires your awareness. By embracing curiosity and optimism in the face of challenges, we pave the way for a mindset shift that becomes a powerful tool in steering through the intricate aspects of personal growth. You are the master of your mind. Let's take a look at how it all starts with your thoughts.

From Thoughts to Action

According to the Cleveland Clinic *Healthy Brains Initiative*, our brains generate over seventy thousand thoughts daily.[2] Our thoughts originate from our senses, memories, beliefs, experiences, and internal dialogues. While the quantity of thoughts varies for each person, it's influenced by many other factors like our mental state, external stimuli, and individual circumstances.

It shouldn't be shocking that the number of thoughts we have a day has grown considerably in the last decade, given the overwhelming amount of information we are exposed to. The overscheduled calendars, technological advancements, and increased connectivity have introduced a flood of stimuli into our day. These factors can lead to a more active thought process, contributing to feelings of overwhelm, anxiousness, and urgency.

In conversations with women, they often tell me, "I feel like I can't keep up."

I'll ask, "Keep up with what?"

The most common reply: "Everything!"

I get it. As women, navigating our complex daily lives with the influx of things coming at us and juggling numerous responsibilities can leave us spinning and uncertain about where to focus our attention.

Recognizing how our brains function with daily thoughts is valuable, and it's helpful to understand the pattern of how thoughts, emotions, and actions work. Albert Ellis, psychologist, psychotherapist, and the founder of rational emotive behavior therapy (REBT), highlighted the interconnectedness of thoughts, emotions, and behaviors, underscoring how our beliefs shape our emotional responses and subsequent actions.[3]

It's even more valuable to understand that, as humans, our minds tend to lean toward negative thoughts more strongly than positive ones, a phenomenon known as negative thought bias.[4] This bias refers to the tendency of the human mind to give more attention to negative information or experiences than positive ones. Negative bias has been wired into our brains for thousands of years as we have evolved from the perceived threats. It's fascinating how our minds can sometimes wander, either reliving our past or fearing or worrying about our future. These thoughts occur independently of our immediate surroundings or the ongoing events in our lives, showcasing the intricate and sometimes unpredictable nature of our thought processes.

Let's take a moment to consider the thoughts and intense feelings of women like Chris walking into her closet cluttered with her emotions tied to her past experiences, or Kelly asking for a raise with unworthiness and money-related stories surfacing. The negative thought loop prevented them from positively changing these areas of their lives. It wasn't until we spotlighted their thought patterns that they shifted to a positive thought loop to replace the negative one. They were then empowered and took action.

Once they were aware of their negative thought loops, they were able to respond differently, now understanding it was their thoughts trying to keep them safe from making change. They controlled their reality.

Negative thought bias is so prevalent in women's lives, especially around body image. The diet culture puts women into a very unhealthy mental negative thought trap. Maybe you've experienced it? Many of my clients and I have. You decide you're going to go on a diet. You go to your friend's dinner party, saying you won't have any sweets, and then find yourself unable to resist and indulge in a plate of dessert. The negative bias may make you think, "I've ruined my entire diet now; I might as well give up." To top that off, we may label our choices as "bad" and even go to the length of announcing it to women at the party. This type of thinking can foster a sense of failure, making it challenging to bounce back and continue with healthier choices. We may even take the label on as being bad. These thoughts and this kind of language can create or reinforce self-defeating thoughts and diminish our worth.

This pattern isn't exclusive to food. It can extend to exercise, rest, sleep, career, your abilities as a mom, and even your to-do list. You name it. I refer to it as the "all-or-nothing" trap, where the negative thought loop gets us into a mindset believing that if you haven't done something with 100 percent of your efforts, you perceive it as a failure or question your actions or effort if you can't give it your all.

Understanding the thought-emotion-action loop is crucial for deciphering the results you experience. Negative bias might be the obstacle preventing you from living your desired life. So, let's work on creating new pathways for success, whether it's the job you want, the weight you want to lose, a better relationship with your partner, or feeling more confident in yourself. The great news is that you can create a new pathway in your brain for success by taking control of your thoughts and emotions and taking intentional steps to shape your reality to achieve your goals. Mindset truly is everything!

Creating New Pathways for Success

When we engage in activities that challenge and push us outside our comfort zones, we stimulate the growth of new neural pathways. This process, known as neuroplasticity, allows us to acquire new knowledge, develop new skills, and improve our cognitive abilities.[5] By consistently engaging in activities that require us to learn and adapt, we can enhance our brain's capacity for growth and development.

In chapter 5, we identified some common self-limiting beliefs and shared strategies and tools to help reframe those beliefs. Sharing my personal experience, I recounted the lingering impact of self-doubt rooted in my ACT results, influencing my perception of standardized tests and my belief in myself for years. Similar struggles with my respiratory boards and a second attempt fueled my negative thought loops even more. Taking my health coaching board exam, I recognized the need to reframe my thoughts. I engaged in activities that challenged my comfort zone and fostered growth. Crucial support from a supportive community, an accountability partner, and a dedicated coach, combined with structured study plans, strategic scheduling, and prioritizing self-care, played a pivotal role in reshaping my mindset and ultimately achieving success. Through intentional efforts, I forged a new neural pathway geared towards success when facing the exam. And it made all the difference.

Creating new neural pathways enhances problem-solving ability, thinking creatively, and making informed decisions. It helps us overcome obstacles and find innovative solutions to challenges. When we challenge our brains and expose ourselves to new experiences, including new thoughts, we expand our perspectives and better understand our world around us. As we develop a more diverse network of neural connections, we become more adaptable, open-minded, and capable of embracing change.

So, are you ready to start creating new neural pathways for your success? The power of visualization can profoundly impact neuroplasticity. Visualization is when you use your imagination to create a mental picture of something you want to achieve or experience. Creating vivid mental images of confidently overcoming challenges and attaining desired outcomes helps reinforce your self-belief and trains your mind to focus on positive possibilities. As we repeatedly visualize these optimistic scenarios, our brain starts to rewire itself, forging new connections and reinforcing the desired thoughts and beliefs.

I have a longer visualization practice you can try later in this chapter, but for now, take a few moments to visualize yourself confidently living your day with intention. Pick one of your goals, close your eyes, and imagine doing it successfully. Imagine yourself going through the motions and being successful in achieving it. Maybe it's experiencing a morning routine that flows with ease, eating nourishing foods that energize you, delivering a presentation to land that promotion, rocking that interview, getting that job you want, or completing that 5K race you've had on your bucket list.

I use visualization often, which worked for me when preparing to take my board exam. I imagined myself taking the test, feeling confident, and even opening the email with results that said,

"Congratulations! You've passed!" Whatever you are working towards, imagine the feelings of accomplishment, pride, and self-assurance that come with your success and feel that energy start to fuel your goal. Use all your senses to step into that future version of yourself, living and achieving what you want. It all starts with empowering thoughts.

The Mindset of Allowing Yourself to Rest

Why are we talking about rest again? We may know what we should be doing to rest, and I've given you some examples of different ways to look at rest, but now we're going to dive into the mindset of rest and what it takes to give ourselves permission to rest. When we do rest, we open up many more possibilities for us.

Let me tell you how Anna reframed her thoughts to allow herself to incorporate rest into her day. Anna had always been caught up in her thoughts that she needed to constantly be on the move, accomplishing one task after another. Even when she returned home in the evenings after a long day at work, her mind raced with the endless to-do list, leaving little room for anything else, especially rest. She had a difficult time unbusying her mind.

Whenever Anna attempted to take a few moments to relax, she was overwhelmed with guilt and restlessness. She would try to spend some time with her husband in the evening to watch a TV show together and, within a short time, she found herself back in the kitchen cleaning out a drawer or making a grocery list for the weekend family event she was hosting. The ingrained belief that being busy equated to being productive haunted her.

"I try to sit still, but I just can't. I don't know why," she told me.

In our coaching session, we discussed unlearning the habit of busyness and reframing her thoughts and mindset around rest. After some questions, we discovered that Anna's idea about rest was reinforced by the messages she'd received when she was younger. Her parents were hard workers and came from a family of immigrants who had to work hard to put food on the table to care for their large family. Anna shared that it was a loving family, but her parents often called her lazy when she didn't complete her household chores.

"We never rested just to take a break. We didn't rest until everything was done."

For Anna, this translated to the strong beliefs and adopting the mindset of:

"Rest = You're lazy."

"You don't get to rest until your work is done."

This mindset was deeply embedded and followed her from childhood into middle age. Guilt settled in from these thoughts, and the "all-or-nothing" approach took a toll on her health, leading her to seek help from her medical provider when she felt so fatigued while struggling to navigate menopause. Her doctor addressed her hormone imbalance and advised her to learn how to handle her stress better. She knew she needed to start listening to her body and allowing herself to rest was a big hurdle she had to overcome.

Together, we explored what would help Anna find a new balance in her life. We moved forward with working on Anna's thoughts about rest while introducing the concept of "snack-size" rest breaks. We eased Anna into embracing relaxation in her day by changing her thoughts about rest.

Teaching your body to rest is a practice, and just as important is training your mind to do the same. Your thoughts play a vital role in unlearning the patterns of busyness, and reframing thoughts to include your benefits of rest is helpful. Incorporating rest into your routine is a valuable practice that creates a nourishing space for your mind, body, and soul. You can show up more powerfully and see possibilities when you are fully energized from rest.

As we continued to meet each week, Anna admitted her thoughts around rest were shifting, but she shared that she didn't give herself time to enjoy a lunch break or even slow down to have regular bathroom breaks at her job. She knew this wasn't good for her body and was ready to implement some changes. We discussed what the benefits of resting and not resting were for her. She began to see the advantages of resting far outweighed the benefits of not resting. So we strategized how she could incorporate taking a thirty-minute lunch break from the office and two five-minute breaks to go to the restroom and practice deep breathing. After just a week of trying her new strategy, she noticed she was more focused and less tired at the end of the day. She made better choices with her food and found that she slept better.

I asked her, "What do you think helped?"

Anna replied, "I realized I often resisted taking breaks, thinking it would slow me down. I was feeling more stressed and tired. It made a significant difference when I started focusing on the benefits of rest and used the breaks to decompress."

Curious, I asked, "Did you notice anything else?"

"I felt more energized when I returned to work and noticed I wasn't craving as much sugar," she shared.

"What do you think made the difference, and did you learn anything from it?"

"I made an agreement with myself that I would only pick two things to focus on completing when I got home, and then I would enjoy some time with my husband. I still had things on my to-do list but realized I didn't have to finish everything," Anna replied with a look of contentment and relief.

When those gremlins of feeling guilty, not being worthy, or not doing enough would appear, Anna recognized them as part of her old stories trying to stop her from resting. The journey wasn't always easy, with moments of resistance and self-doubt. That's when she leaned into understanding that her thoughts were trying to hijack her attempt to rest.

Having support from me and our community of women in the group coaching program reminded her that rest was what she needed to help her stay true to her goals. Through it all, Anna learned the power of recognizing her old thoughts about rest, self-compassion, and adopting the mindset that rest is good for her body and her mind. Taking small steps for positive change and experiencing the benefits helped reinforce a new perspective on rest.

During one of our coaching sessions, Anna's revelation was powerful as she declared to the group, "I am deserving of rest."

This shift in mindset unfolded a cascade of positive possibilities for her. Through rest, she gained better focus, productivity, and patience to become a more composed and calm presence at work and home. Anna realized that embracing rest wasn't a sign of weakness but a source of strength, allowing her to be the best version of herself for herself, her family, and her coworkers.

Ready to break free from the "all-or-nothing" mindset and embrace rest as a possibility generating activity?

Here are six steps to guide you in reframing your mindset around rest.

Step 1: Rethink Rest

Challenge the belief that rest is an all-or-nothing concept. Instead of viewing it as a luxury or something reserved for extended periods, reframe rest as a series of small, rejuvenating moments contributing to your overall well-being.

Step 2: Set "Snack-Size" Goals

Rather than aiming for long stretches of rest, set small, achievable goals for short breaks throughout the day. These could be as brief as five minutes of deep breathing, a quick stretch, or a few moments of mindfulness.

Step 3: Schedule the Breaks

Incorporate rest breaks into your daily schedule. Sprinkle rest into your day by using electronic reminders or productivity apps to prompt you to pause and take a moment for yourself. By scheduling these breaks, you prioritize them as essential components of your routine.

Step 4: Experiment with Curiosity

Explore different kinds and ways to rest to find what works best for you. As we covered in chapter 6, experimentation allows you to discover which type of rest works best for you depending on how you feel.

Step 5: Integrate Mindfully

Mindfully integrate these breaks into your routine. Step away from your work or responsibilities when the reminder prompts you. Fully engage in the rest activity, and savor the rejuvenating moments. Yes, this means removing your distractions including disconnecting from your cell phone.

Step 6: Reflect on the Impact

At the end of each day, take a moment to reflect on how your rest breaks affect how you feel and show up. Notice any changes in energy, focus, or mood? This reflection reinforces the positive impact of incorporating regular, small rest breaks into your routine.

Now It's Your Turn

What "snack-size" rest break will you implement today?
After you try it, did you notice a difference in how you felt?
What possibilities open up when you adopt the mindset that rest is a powerful part of your routine?

By approaching rest in bite-sized increments, it's possible to cultivate a mindset that sees rest as a powerful practice to relieve stress, feel more centered and focused, and see your possibilities more clearly.

Self-Care = Self-Love = Self-Belief

Tracy had never considered the language and thoughts she had about herself. During our coaching calls, she used phrases like, "I hate how my body looks." "I wish I had a body like hers," or "I'm so fat."

I stopped her when she was in a full assault on herself and said, "Tracy, do you always talk about yourself this way?"

Looking shocked, she replied, "I guess I never noticed it."

As we navigated her story, we discussed when and where these thoughts might have come from.

Tears welled up in Tracy's eyes as she realized, "Growing up surrounded by my two sisters and my mom, we had frequent conversations about body image. Most of our discussions were riddled with negativity about ourselves."

Tracy agreed it highlighted the need to break free from her negative self-talk and was ready to cultivate a mindset grounded in self-love and compassion. She admitted it affected her relationship with food and seeped into how she cared for herself. This realization prompted Tracy to confront the programmed patterns she had been running in her mind. The key to her transformation wasn't solely physical but extended to the depths of how she loved herself.

Learning to believe in herself and recognizing her inherent worth became pivotal for Tracy as she changed her relationship with her body. After a few months, she had a good meal plan, nourishing herself with good foods, and practicing self-care by carving out time on her calendar to enjoy morning walks before work. After more conversations about ways to show herself some love, we brainstormed some ideas. One of the ideas was writing a love letter to herself. As uncomfortable and maybe silly as it sounded, she was open to trying it.

As we discussed her love letter in her next session, I asked Tracy, "Would you like to share what you learned writing a love letter to yourself?"

"It was so powerful. Writing to myself with love and kindness felt so different and amazing," she said as a smile came to her face.

"What do you mean by different?" I asked.

Tracy shared, "By writing my love letter, I felt the difference in my thoughts, and it had me feeling empowered rather than defeated. I realized that caring for and loving myself helps me believe in myself."

I responded, affirming, "Self-care = self-love = self-belief."

She laughed and responded with a new look of confidence, "Yes, it's taken me over fifty years, but writing this letter helped me appreciate and love myself for who I am. I am worth it!"

For years, Tracy had grappled with negative self-talk, lacking self-compassion and love in her internal dialogue. But this shift marked the turning point in Tracy's journey toward fostering self-love and acceptance. It exemplified how her beliefs about herself and a sense of worthiness became the foundation for cultivating a positive and nurturing relationship with herself. She rediscovered the value of nourishing herself with good food, self-care, and the right mindset.

A report by *The Body Shop*® in March 2021 revealed a global crisis of low self-love and self-worth among women. The study surveyed over 22,000 participants from 21 countries and found that half of the women felt more self-doubt than self-love, with 60 percent wishing for respect. Factors such as financial status, lack of progress toward goals, and external factors like politics and the economy contributed to low confidence.[6] These findings emphasize the need for our society to cultivate self-acceptance, empowerment, and compassion, creating an environment where women feel valued and can embrace their true worth.

Self-belief and self-love are interconnected and mutually reinforce our self-worth. We trust our abilities, talents, and potential to achieve our goals when we have a strong sense of self-belief. A strong foundation of self-love is essential for developing self-belief. When we love and accept ourselves, we create an environment where self-belief can thrive. We build self-confidence and self-assurance by acknowledging our inherent worth and treating ourselves with kindness, compassion, and respect.

One of the critical ways self-belief influences our personal growth is by fostering a mindset of resilience and perseverance. When we have a strong sense of self-belief, we are likelier to take risks, step out of our comfort zones, take action, and make decisions. Self-belief influences the way we handle setbacks and failures. Instead of viewing them as reflections of our worth or abilities, we see them as temporary setbacks on our journey to success. We understand that failure is an essential part of growth and learning, and we use it as an opportunity to gain valuable insights and improve ourselves.

Failure does not need to be viewed as a failure. Instead, embracing that there is no such thing as failure, only feedback, I'm either winning or I'm learning, is a healthy and loving perspective to adopt. When we practice self-love, we recognize our worthiness and embrace our imperfections. We prioritize self-care, setting boundaries and engaging in activities that nourish our well-being. Sound familiar? Self-love is taking your turn and saying "yes" to you!

Writing a love letter to yourself is a beautiful and empowering exercise. You can follow Tracy's steps to create a heartfelt letter that celebrates your value, reinforces your self-belief, and encourages self-love. As you engage in this exercise, remember that self-love is an act of kindness to yourself and a profound form of self-care. Light a candle, play some soothing music, or surround yourself with things that bring you joy and let your words flow.

Here are the steps to write a love letter to yourself.

Step 1: Connect with Compassion

Close your eyes and take a few deep breaths before you get started. Take a few moments to reflect on your positive qualities, what makes you unique and your achievements. Consider moments of strength, resilience, and kindness.

Step 2: Write a Love Letter

Begin by expressing gratitude for who you are. Acknowledge your strengths, talents, and the challenges you've overcome. Celebrate who you are, your journey and growth.

Step 3: Encourage and Affirm

Write words of encouragement and support to yourself. Remind yourself of your capabilities and potential. Encourage self-compassion and acknowledge that it's okay to be imperfect.

Step 4: Vision for Your Future You

Consider what self-love means to you. Reflect on how you can actively cultivate self-love in your daily life. Envision a future where you continue to grow, love yourself more deeply, and embrace your worth. Write about the positive changes you foresee in your journey.

Step 5: Seal It With Love

Conclude your letter with a loving closing. Consider sealing it with a kiss, a positive affirmation, or any symbol representing self-love.

Step 6: Read It Aloud

Once you've finished your letter, read it aloud to yourself. Allow the words to resonate and feel the positive energy you've created. Embrace the love and encouragement you've shared.

Remember, this is a personal and intimate exercise, so let your heart guide your words and take the time you need. Take it one step at a time.

Now It's Your Turn

How did it feel to extend compassion and love to yourself during this exercise?
As you wrote your love letter, did you notice any shifts in how you feel about yourself?
How can you show love for yourself each day, much like you might show your best friend?

Creating Your Abundance

My friend Claire and I met when our families were stationed in Okinawa, Japan, in 2015. We hadn't talked that often over the last few years, but one particular day, I was thinking of her. So I picked up the phone and gave her a call.

"Shari!" I could tell she was surprised to hear from me.

We immediately jumped into our conversation, exchanging updates on our kids and husbands, and then the conversation shifted to how we were doing. Claire was caught juggling work, family, and other responsibilities with her parents' health deteriorating. She spoke about the constant demands on her time and energy, leaving her feeling drained and overwhelmed.

Taking a moment for herself seemed like an indulgence she couldn't afford. She opened up about the persistent stress and fatigue she felt. When I asked about how she was taking care of herself, she shared that her idea of allocating time and resources for self-care was a foreign concept, clouded by notions of guilt and scarcity. I appreciated her words as it was how I felt a few years earlier. I opened up about my journey, expressing regret for neglecting my self-care.

As I went into the details of the roller coaster of my symptoms, medical appointments, and how my experience led me to get healthier, she asked, "How do I change my thoughts and feelings about spending time on myself? I feel so guilty even thinking about doing it."

We both acknowledged that the scarcity and unworthiness influenced some of our beliefs and stories we often felt as military spouses not contributing financially to our households.

As a friend, I shared, "Our thoughts are wired to look for the negative or lack in our lives. I had to start by looking at what the benefits would be if I started taking care of myself. Then, when I did it, I felt the benefits far outweighed depriving or neglecting my care."

"I never really thought about how we are wired like that. It's so true. How can I change my thoughts about spending money on myself?" Claire asked.

I shared, "When you invest time or money, you're not throwing it away. You're exchanging it for something of value to you. I had to change my mindset and language. Instead of using the word 'spending' time or money, I swapped it out to say, 'investing' instead."

Claire listened intently, absorbing the idea that caring for oneself is not throwing something away but exchanging resources for something profoundly valuable.

"Oh, wow, when you put it that way, it makes sense and sounds much better," she said.

"Yeah, as I was forced to invest in my health, I saw the benefits that returned in a much bigger way. I started looking at the abundance that came to me and my family when I changed my thoughts about investing in myself with resources."

As we wrapped up our conversation, we wished each other well and promised to be better about checking in more frequently. Claire promised me she would try to take better care of herself.

Fostering an abundance mindset is a powerful perspective that embraces the belief that opportunities, resources, and possibilities are readily available. It is a mindset rooted in gratitude, optimism, and a deep sense of abundance rather than scarcity.

By practicing gratitude and acknowledging abundance, we cultivate a sense of contentment and fulfillment. We begin to see opportunities where we once saw obstacles, and we approach challenges with a mindset of possibility rather than limitation. This mindset allows us to tap into our creativity and resourcefulness, finding innovative solutions and opening doors to new experiences.

When we look at our health and well-being, an abundance mindset transforms how we perceive investments in ourselves. Regular medical checkups stop being viewed as expenses and instead become proactive steps towards living a longer, healthier life. Nutrient-rich foods are not just groceries; they are investments in our daily fuel, nurturing both body and mind. Gym memberships and fitness classes evolve into investments in our physical strength and overall health. Allocating time and resources for mental health activities, like therapy or mindfulness practices, is an investment in our emotional well-being. Quality sleep and relaxation are not luxuries but vital investments in heightened productivity and feeling more energy. Personal development workshops and well-being practices, from massages to health classes, are seen not as expenditures but as indispensable investments enriching our health.

In my situation, I realized the value of prioritizing self-care: a healthier body and a new commitment to allowing myself the care I deserve.

A few months later, I got a call from Claire, who thanked me because she'd taken our conversation to heart and embraced her self-care differently after our discussion.

"There was one thing you said that impacted me. Money and time are an exchange of what we value," she said.

Claire followed with an update, "I've carved out moments in my schedule for activities that bring me joy and relaxation—a massage, an afternoon walk in nature, and even a weekend retreat for me and my husband to recharge."

Initially hesitant, Claire shared that the regular massages became a sanctuary of rejuvenation, easing the tension she carried in her shoulders and providing respite from the demands of daily life. The walks in nature became a cherished ritual, offering moments of calm to clear her mind. The weekend getaway for her and her husband, which initially seemed extravagant, was a priceless investment for their mental and emotional health and strengthened their relationship.

"I've learned that self-care is not an act of selfishness but a necessary exchange for balance and peace," Claire said with a calmness in her voice.

The shift in her mindset—from viewing self-care as a luxury to recognizing it as a valuable investment—profoundly impacted her well-being. Claire's story serves as a testament to the liberating truth that taking care of herself is a priceless exchange that fuels her abundance.

If you find it hard to invest time or money on your needs like Claire and me, let's have some fun playing *The Fifty Ways for Self-Care Game,* designed to shift your perspective on investing time and money in self-care. As you explore various ways to nurture yourself, use this as a powerful tool to break free from a scarcity mindset and embrace a more abundant and fulfilling life through self-love and care. The idea is not that you have to do all fifty ways, but that you are opening your mind to think of what could be possible.

Now It's Your Turn

Here are the steps to play The Fifty Ways for Self-Care Game:

Step 1: Generate ideas.

Start brainstorming a list of self-care actions or activities that bring you joy, enhance your well-being, and contribute to your overall abundance. For this exercise, don't let time or money block you from writing the idea down. The idea of fifty ways is that you challenge yourself to see how many possible ways there are, no matter the investment.

Step 2: Think broad.

Ensure your abundance list includes a variety of self-care practices, covering physical, mental, emotional, spiritual, and social aspects of your well-being.

Step 3: The feeling is the magnet.

As you create your list, pay attention to the emotional impact of each self-care action. Note how each activity makes you feel—does it make you feel calm, energized, excited, joyful, or fulfilled?

Step 4: List your benefit.

List your benefit next to each idea.
What is the payoff for you or others when you do that activity?

> ### Step 5: Focus on one and go!
> *Taking action is how to get comfortable investing time or money into self-care. So, pick one thing and turn your self-care idea into a specific, actionable goal. For example, instead of a general statement like "exercise," specify it as "take a thirty-minute nature walk four times this week" or "try a new fitness class this week."*

Recognize and celebrate small wins. Even seemingly minor self-care actions can have a profound effect on how you feel and can open your mind to even more possibilities. Cultivate a mindset that appreciates and acknowledges your efforts to create even more abundance!

Believing in Yourself and Your Vision

One of my favorite shows is *Ted Lasso*, a comedy-drama television show that revolves around an American college football coach, Ted Lasso, played by Jason Sudeikis. Ted is hired to lead the struggling English Premier League soccer team, AFC Richmond. The show dives into diverse themes such as sportsmanship, leadership, and relationships. Renowned for its unique blend of humor and poignant character development, *Ted Lasso* skillfully navigates the complexities of the characters' lives.

In one scene from season three, episode ten, Rebecca Welton (the team's owner, portrayed by Hannah Waddingham), is preparing for a crucial owners' meeting with a room full of overconfident men. As she gets dressed, it's evident that her thoughts are getting the best of her, shaking her confidence. Rebecca proceeds to do a breathing exercise to try to calm herself. Then she does something so powerful. She walks over to a full-sized mirror, closes her eyes, and takes a deep breath, placing her hands over her heart. Opening her eyes, she envisions her younger self in the mirror, smiling at her. She smiles back. Then she bends over, takes a deep breath, and stands back up with her arms outstretched, letting out her air with a lion's breath. Through this power exercise, she metaphorically "makes herself big," tapping into the transformative potential of visualization.

After using this approach, she is transformed into a more confident and empowered version of herself. It was a beautiful moment of compassion, remembering who she was and feeling her strength. She enters the meeting and stands in her power by displaying her grace and confidence in the face of the challenge. Of all the episodes, this is my favorite moment in the show because it demonstrates the power of our thoughts and what can happen in just a few minutes when we believe in ourselves.

We create our reality based on what we believe. For far too long, we've bought into the saying "seeing is believing," so we only do something if we see it in our world. It can be difficult to "see" our vision. But when we believe in our vision and start taking action from believing rather than seeing, we get results: from thinking to feeling to action. There is that thought-emotion-action loop again.

In his book, *The Biology of Belief*, author Bruce H. Lipton discusses the relationship between beliefs and the subconscious mind and its impact on shaping our perceptions and experiences.[7] Our brain doesn't know the difference between the reality of something happening or not. But with visualization, we create the feeling as if it has. We build belief in ourselves by vividly imagining ourselves as if the goal or thing we want has already happened. As I mentioned, we can use visualization for any of our goals.

228 IT'S YOUR TURN

Now It's Your Turn

*Here is a more extended version of a visualization.
Give it a try!*

Close your eyes and take a deep breath. Imagine yourself waking up in the morning feeling refreshed and energized. Picture yourself getting out of bed with excitement for the day ahead. You lace up your shoes, feeling your body becoming more awake and alive by moving your body with an early morning walk outside breathing the cool air. Feel the satisfaction of engaging in a movement that you enjoy. As you go through your morning routine, see yourself making conscious choices that nourish your body and mind. Visualize preparing a nutritious breakfast that fuels you for the day. You're not rushed. You are fueling yourself first to be the person you want to be today. You get ready and feel more energetic and prepared to take on your day.

Now, imagine yourself throughout the day, making mindful choices that support your health. Visualize yourself staying hydrated, enjoying the lunch you prepared with foods that give you energy, and taking breaks to stretch and breathe deeply. You attend the meetings on your schedule and feel focused on your work. After a meeting, you need to stretch, so you walk outside during your afternoon break and feel the warm sunshine on your face. Choosing a nourishing snack, you take a few deep breaths and feel a sense of calm and balance as you manage any stress, knowing you have the tools to handle it.

Picture yourself as you wrap up your day of work with a clutter-free desk, organized with the items you like to see arranged, and a calendar that shows the tasks you'll start with tomorrow morning. All your work gets to stay right there. It's safe—no need to take it home. You end the day with a sense of accomplishment and contentment, knowing you're the person you want to be by doing what you need to feel nourished and happy. Now slowly come back to this present moment, wiggle your fingers and toes and open your eyes. Carry this visualization with you as a reminder of your goal. Remember that each choice is a step towards creating more balance and calm.

Now, this was a short example of how you can use the power of visualization to help you believe in having a smooth day filled with energy. Visualization is a powerful tool that can increase your motivation and confidence. Believing in your vision and feeling worthy provides the foundation for turning your goals into reality. This can fuel your determination and the courage to pursue your dreams with an unwavering commitment.

Celebrate Every Step of the Way

Sarah had been working consistently on adopting healthier habits and achieved a significant milestone—losing fifteen pounds. She received the exciting news when she visited her doctor for a checkup. Her doctor was ecstatic, as her success was even more apparent in her bloodwork results, which showed her blood sugar had improved. It was a significant accomplishment that filled Sarah with pride and satisfaction.

She shared her celebration with me, and I was so excited for her. I reminded her to share her celebration with the women in our text chat within the coaching group. Sarah felt conflicted. She told me she didn't want to boast or brag when sharing her successes with the other women in our group. When we started exploring this further, we hit on something.

She admitted, "I remember a time when I shared winning a competition with my best friend in high school. After I did that, she told me I shouldn't be such a show-off. I never really liked to share anything with anyone after that."

Recognizing Sarah's hesitation, I reassured her that celebrating her win was essential, no matter how small or big. I reminded her that the purpose of the celebration was not to boast or make others feel inadequate. Instead, it was about acknowledging who she was, her power, and how her hard work helped her reach her goal. Celebrating her success would honor her efforts, and in the right community circle, it would inspire and motivate others.

With gentle encouragement, she shared her celebration. It was a beautiful thing to witness because of the spark that ignited her confidence for many other celebrations to follow. The community of women was her fuel for growth, and she was the fuel for the group. Many of the members shared positive comments, like, "I'm so excited for you, Sarah; you inspire me to keep going with my goals too!"

Engaging with supportive friends, mentors, or a community of like-minded individuals who uplift and inspire you becomes your vibration in which your mind and body operates. Your tribe is your vibe, and your vibration attracts your tribe. The more you hang out with those living your vision, the more you will think it's possible.

Regular conversations with them, sharing your goals and challenges, and receiving their guidance and support will counteract self-doubt and provide a nurturing environment for personal growth. In all of life's demands and expectations, it's easy to forget just how powerful the impact of our relationships is on us. Celebrating these victories reinforces your self-belief and builds momentum for further growth.

I encourage my clients to share and celebrate their weekly wins. This practice serves as a powerful motivator to keep them going on their journey toward their goals. It also helps them recognize that they often underestimate or overlook their accomplishments.

Too often, we downplay our successes, focusing solely on what's next. Taking the time to acknowledge and celebrate your accomplishments helps maintain your motivation, boost self-confidence, and foster a positive mindset. Embrace the practice of celebrating both big and small wins. Recognize that each step forward, no matter how small, contributes to your overall progress. Whether reaching a milestone, overcoming a challenge, or making one positive change, give yourself permission to celebrate and bask in the joy of your achievements.

The power to choose our influences and cultivate supportive relationships lies within us. By surrounding ourselves with positive influences, nurturing supportive relationships, and actively engaging in a community of like-minded individuals, we create fertile ground for personal empowerment, growth, and self-care. Together, we can create a ripple effect of positive change in our lives and the lives of those around us.

Now It's Your Turn

What small steps do you need to acknowledge you've taken towards bigger goals?

> *What are you most proud of?*
> *What will you do to celebrate your wins?*

The Power of Your Mind Wrap-Up

Your mindset is an incredible muscle that deserves daily strengthening, just like your body. The power of the mind goes beyond adjustments like changing the food we eat or starting an exercise program. It requires an inner transformation.

It was hard to see possibilities during my chaotic Messy Web periods. My thoughts revolved around the never-ending to-do list: "What do I have to do today?" This perpetual focus on always *doing* left no room for introspection about "Who am I being?"

During challenging circumstances, embracing the question of "Who am I being?" may feel elusive. The phrase "it is what it is" became a coping mechanism, acknowledging the reality of my situation and thinking there was no other way. However, I realized that when I started taking care of myself with the mindset that I *get* to take care of myself, I could transform this into my new reality. Taking intentional steps shifted my perspective from focusing on endless tasks to a more profound understanding of who I am and how I want to be in the world. These small steps helped foster my worth and shifted my mindset, supporting and rocketing my personal growth.

As we conclude this chapter, let's take a moment to reflect on the amazing power our thoughts hold in shaping our reality. From understanding the intricate patterns of your thoughts, emotions, and actions to recognizing rest as a possibility generating activity, we've discovered a power within ourselves. Acknowledging our worth and value opens the door to abundance in different aspects of our lives. Celebrating our progress by taking the time to recognize and appreciate every milestone fuels our motivation and cultivates a positive mindset where we can thrive.

Surrounding ourselves with like-minded individuals who uplift and inspire us can provide invaluable support, encouragement, and inspiration. They believe in our potential and will help us thrive on our path to personal growth. The key lies in cultivating a mindset that believes in the future version of ourselves, visualizing the possibilities, and embracing the practice of saying "yes" to our needs and desires. Every positive thought, every act of self-love, and every celebration of your progress is a testament to your belief in yourself. Keep saying "yes" to you, and know that the mindset you're creating is one for a life of abundance, fulfillment, and enormous success.

Chapter 7 Key Takeaways

- We get to decide how we let our circumstances dictate our thoughts, feelings, and actions.

- The thought-emotion-action loop shows us that change starts with how we think, and feeling is the magnet that draws us to take action.

- It's possible to create a new pathway for success through neuroplasticity. Visualization is a powerful tool that can build belief in ourselves.

- Self-care = self-love = self-belief. They are all connected to worthiness.

- Practicing gratitude and fostering an abundant mindset cultivates a sense of fulfillment.

- When we believe in ourselves, we stand in our power and invite others to do the same.

If you would like to practice applying the *It's Your Turn* strategies to your own life, please use your cell phone camera to scan the QR code below or use the hyperlink at https://itsyourturnbook.com/resources.

itsyourturnbook.com/resources

PART III

Chapter 8

Embracing Your Turn and Becoming Alive With Purpose

I am fully present, my mind is clear, and I am focused on what matters most.
—Shari Biery

In the intricate dance of military life, where duty often takes precedence, the journey of a military spouse is marked by substantial sacrifices. The toll is palpable for many women as they find themselves surrendering pieces of their identity with each step—a career relinquished for love, a fit body transformed through motherhood, and even cherished hobbies forgotten by the relentless demands of everyday routines. Staring into the mirror, the reflection appears unfamiliar, feeling confused and lost in the roles of spouse, mom, and supporter. The exhaustion is real, and the yearning for a life beyond the confines of duty becomes profound.

In our daily lives, chronic low-level stress has become an accepted norm woven into the fabric of our existence. Our society glorifies busyness, and the idea that our worth is tied to how much we can accomplish—the hidden sacrifices and burdens we carry as women can be overwhelming. Unfortunately, the emphasis on always being productive and working tirelessly can come at the cost of our well-being. Unchecked stress, if left unaddressed, can lead to severe health issues and, more alarmingly, take precious years from your life.

In my quest for better health, I didn't want a simple "take this pill, and you'll feel better" solution. I wanted to go beyond treating symptoms and find the real reasons behind my health issues. I was determined to understand and heal my body. The guidance of a supportive and compassionate healthcare provider who looked at my health from a whole-body approach and was well-versed in the intricacies of hormonal balance made all the difference for me. This opened my eyes to how our body systems are interconnected and how symptoms can often be traced back to underlying causes. I recognize that many healthcare providers are tied to systems that limit their capability and depend on insurance companies, which can make it difficult to care for patients with different health concerns. As advocates for our health, it's time to take a stand for prevention and a comprehensive approach to our well-being as women.

My provider's approach helped by exploring my issues from a whole-body perspective rather than focusing solely on my symptoms, opening up a world of possibilities. She guided me through dietary changes, focusing on nourishing foods and essential supplements to address my nutrient deficiencies. Along my journey, I uncovered the intricate connections between stress, hormones, and the disruptive impact of lifestyle choices on my hormonal equilibrium. I discovered that managing stress by dedicating time for myself, setting boundaries on work and extra activities, and creating healthy coping strategies helped me feel calmer and more centered.

An adopted phrase in my coaching training was, "You are your first client." As a student, I focused on my health and wellness and began understanding the role certain foods could play in helping my symptoms. I noticed my body's signals when I ate certain foods. This approach significantly boosted my energy and improved my focus and motivation. Understanding the effects of sugar on my body and the influence of stress on my hormonal health became another critical piece of the puzzle. I focused on reducing my refined sugar and processed foods by getting curious and reading labels. By noticing how my body reacted when I had sugary drinks, alcohol, or extra sweets, I started making connections. Moving my body became a habit that I found enjoyable. These were pivotal steps in restoring harmony and reclaiming control over my body. I went from feeling trapped and hopeless to empowered and alive.

This journey emphasized the significance of self-care and illuminated the profound impact of my lifestyle choices on my hormonal balance and overall well-being. I embraced the concept of being curious and letting go of judgment. This empowering path of self-awareness and self-care has transformed my life and fostered more robust relationships with my husband, kids, family, and friends. And, most importantly, I've created a deeper connection with myself by leaning into my spirituality and believing that God has a real purpose for me and my gifts.

I've done the work and tuned into the roadblocks holding me back from taking my turn. This heightened awareness persisted even after my husband retired from military service. I've realized that my body holds onto the memories and experiences of those tumultuous times, and it's my responsibility to take ownership of it and face it for my health.

The burden of stress from the memories and experiences, quietly borne by many of us, takes a toll on our bodies and often goes unnoticed. As I navigated emotions like unworthiness, guilt, and resentment, I realized the antidote was stepping up even more to take care of myself.

By learning to live in the present moment and deciding each day who I get to be, I continue to do my work by declaring what I want in my life and then celebrating each step I take.

Despite showcasing remarkable strength through sacrifices, now is the time to shape a new story for you—one where prioritizing self-care triumphs over self-sacrifice. It's entirely within your grasp. You can take care of yourself while also bringing brightness into the lives of others. Think of this moment as a fresh chapter, transforming into a guiding light for those who look up to you. Remember, you must keep adding fuel to your light to ensure it continues to burn brightly. Embrace this opportunity to be alive with purpose, contributing to your well-being and illuminating the path for those around you.

In sharing my story, the stories of my clients, and the tools of my C.A.L.M. method within these pages, my intention is not for this book to collect dust on a shelf. Instead, my wish is that you use it as a reference, a guide you can turn to whenever you need a reminder, an exercise, or a strategy to take care of yourself. I hope you carry this book with you, not just in your hands but in your heart, as a source of inspiration and empowerment whenever you need it. You hold the power to emerge from your challenges stronger, wiser, and with a renewed sense of purpose.

I'm a different woman today, shaped by the experiences I've been through. Writing these words validates my experience. I hope my vulnerability helps you gain permission to acknowledge and validate yours too. If your body is trying to tell you something, don't ignore it. Listen and take action.

By acknowledging this, you get to transform your pain into purpose, turn invisible sacrifices into visible triumphs, foster resilience from resentment, gain clarity from overwhelm, and strengthen unshakeable self-worth, dispelling any lingering feelings of unworthiness.

The ability to shape your path is firmly in your hands. Step into your power, embrace your journey, and live with purpose. Your story doesn't end here—it's your next chapter of a new beginning. Embrace your turn!

Quick Reference Guide for the C.A.L.M. Method

Step 1: Clarity

Chapter 4: Clarity is Your Compass

- The Gift of the Pause - Clarify What You Truly Desire

- The Art of Being - Living into Who You Want to Be

- Finding Your Big Why - Understand Your Reasons Behind Your Desires

- Values in Action - Identify Your Values Celebrating You

- Create Your Vision - Examine the Five Big Areas of Your Life to Establish Your Goals

Step 2: Awareness

Chapter 5: Awareness of What's Slowing You Down

- Creating Time - Reclaim Your Time by Using the *Time Journal Tool*

- Establishing Boundaries - Master Saying "Yes" or "No" Using the *Priority Power-Up Practice*

- Releasing Control - Using the *It's the Who, Not You Practice* to Lighten Your Load

- People Pleasing - Learning How to Say "No" to Say "Yes" to You

- Recognizing Your Value - Claim Your Value by Unveiling Your Worth

- Money Beliefs - Recognizing Money Stories to Build Your Worthiness

- Belief in Yourself - Build Confidence and Believe in Yourself

Step 3: Learning

Chapter 6: Learning to Listen to Your Body

- The Connection of Stress, Sugar, and Hormones - *B.A.U.—Breathe, Access, Unload*

- A Clear Space is a Clear Mind - Clearing the Clutter

- Answering Your Craving for Rest - Establish a Consistent Rest Routine

- The Power of Strong Social Connections - Enhance Your Social Connections

- Consistent Nourishment with Meal Planning - Strategies for Planning Your Meals

- Eating What Is Right for You - Creating Your Balanced Plate

- Moving Your Body - Discovering Your Favorite Movement

- Embracing the Healing Power of Sleep - Essential Components for Quality Sleep

Step 4: Mindset

Chapter 7: Mindset of Saying "Yes" to Yourself

- Rest is a Possibility Generating Activity - Adopting "Snack-Size" Rest

- Self-Love is Self-Care - The Words You Deserve To Hear With A Love Letter To You

- Create Your Abundance - Developing 50 Ways To Create Self-Care

- Believe in Yourself - Future Version of You & the Power of Visualization

- Celebrate Every Step of the Way - No Matter How Small or Big

Bonus Materials

Y ou took your turn by reading this book and implementing the practices in the C.A.L.M. method. You are part of a movement that encourages and values women to care for themselves.

In my coaching programs, I facilitate the C.A.L.M. method directly, and I want you to have as close to that experience as possible. If you would like to practice applying the *It's Your Turn* strategies to your own life, I've created an online book portal with bonus resources and ways to join the community to help you. Please use your cell phone camera to scan the QR code below or use the hyperlink at https://itsyourturnbook.com/resources.

itsyourturnbook.com/resources

Book Club Guide

The power of community has been a guiding light in my journey, offering support through challenges and celebrating victories. It's a truth I've come to hold dear—we don't thrive in isolation but in community.

I've surrounded myself with visionaries, mission-driven women, and insightful coaches and mentors who've illuminated my path and helped me navigate my blind spots. Standing at the intersection of your wellness and purpose, I encourage you to seek your community.

Implement the strategies shared in this book by engaging with supportive friends, mentors, or joining a community of like-minded individuals. Your journey is uniquely yours, but it's enriched when shared. Your community will be your sounding board, support system, and your source of inspiration.

Your journey towards a purposeful and balanced life doesn't end here; it evolves. Embrace the tools, mindset shifts, and practices you've discovered. In the online book portal, you can find a guide I created especially for you to help facilitate your book club.

You can find this guide in the *It's Your Turn* Resource Book Portal at https://itsyourturnbook.com/resources.

itsyourturnbook.com/resources

Favorite Resources

Health & Wellness

NBHWC: Find a health coach
https://nbhwc.org/what-is-a-health-coach

Osteopathic Medicine: Find a DO
https://findado.osteopathic.org

Institute for Functional Medicine
https://www.ifm.org/find-a-practitioner

The American Academy of Anti-Aging Medicine (A4M)
https://www.a4m.com/find-a-doctor.html

Mental Health

Better Help
https://www.betterhelp.com/about

National Alliance on Mental Illness
https://www.nami.org/help

Military Spouse Resources

"Once a Milspouse, Always a Milspouse."

In writing this book, I discovered valuable resources and programs that champion and support our military families. Employment is a crucial aspect of stability for military spouses, and I am dedicated to advocating for opportunities that empower and uplift this community. By sharing these resources, my goal is to contribute to the well-being and professional growth of military spouses around the world. While there are many organizations available, this is not an exhaustive list. These are some of my favorite.

Military OneSource is a program that provides a wide range of support and resources for active-duty military members, National Guard and Reserve members, and their families. It is a Department of Defense funded program that offers confidential nonmedical counseling, information, and resources on various topics to help military families navigate the unique challenges of military life.
To learn more visit:
https://www.militaryonesource.mil

ACT Now Education provides opportunities and support for active duty personnel, veterans, reservists, the National Guard, military spouses, and dependents.
To learn more visit:
https://actnoweducation.org

AMSE (Association of Military Spouse Entrepreneurs) connects military spouse business owners with the tools and resources needed to become successful in launching and growing their businesses.
To learn more visit:
https://amseagency.com

Blue Star Families is a nonprofit organization that provides support, resources, and programs for military families. Blue Star Families offers a variety of initiatives, including community events, wellness programs, career development resources, and efforts to address the unique challenges faced by military families.
To learn more visit:
https://bluestarfam.org

Hiring Our Heroes is a program initiated by the US Chamber of Commerce Foundation with the aim of assisting veterans, transitioning service members, and military spouses in finding meaningful employment opportunities. The program offers a range of services, including career fairs, networking events, mentorship programs, and resources to connect military-affiliated individuals with potential employers.
To learn more visit:
https://www.hiringourheroes.org

InDependent is a wellness community for military spouses built by military spouses.
To learn more visit:
https://in-dependent.org

Joining Forces focuses on key areas such as employment, education, and wellness for military veterans and their families.

To learn more visit:

https://www.whitehouse.gov/joiningforces

Military Spouse Chamber of Commerce assists military spouses considering entrepreneurship, business ownership, or freelancing as a career. Join the Military Spouse Chamber for free.

To learn more visit:

https://milspousechamber.org/membership

Military Spouse Advocacy Network is a robust network of advocates, mentors, and volunteers serving our military families and improving the morale and welfare of our communities through education, empowerment, support, community, and collaboration.

To learn more visit:

https://www.militaryspouseadvocacynetwork.org

National Military Spouse Network is a networking, mentoring and professional development organization committed to the education, empowerment, and advancement of military spouses.

To learn more visit:

https://www.nationalmilitaryspousenetwork.org

Twelve Million Plus is a digital community for military and veteran spouses to connect with other military spouses around the world.

To learn more visit:

https://www.twelvemillionplus.com

Acknowledgments

As I share *It's Your Turn* with the world, my heart is overflowing with gratitude for each of you who has played a role in making this book come alive.

To You, The Reader,
May this book be a source of inspiration, empowerment, and endless possibilities. Remember, you're capable of amazing things! Believe in yourself!

To My Clients, Both Former and Present,
I am grateful for the privilege of accompanying you on your unique journey. Your trust and commitment to growth are the driving force behind our work together. Thank you for allowing me to be a part of the valuable lessons you've shared, enriching your lives and mine.

To Sara,
This all started with your question, "Do you have a book in you that could help someone and change their life?" You are an incredible coach. Thank you for believing in my vision and mission, especially when I wasn't sure if it would happen. You kept me focused on my path knowing "I can and I will."

To My Talented Editors, Hannah, Audrey, and Lisa,
Your commitment to helping me improve my craft and deepening my love for writing has made me a better writer and elevated the overall quality of this book. Working with

you has been an enriching experience, and I could not have done it without you. Thank you for being instrumental in bringing this book to its fullest potential.

To Tracy,
Your words of affirmation were a beacon of encouragement that guided me through writing this book. Your heartfelt plea, "Please, write the book!" to address the fatigue experienced by women supporting their high-achieving spouses and families became a driving force behind every word. Thank you for being a source of strength and inspiration, especially when I wasn't sure I wanted to keep going.

To Kristine,
From the moment I hired you to create the logo for my business to today, it has been an incredible adventure with you. Thank you for crafting the beautiful book cover. Your creative talent, sage advice, and honest conversations have been priceless. Beyond the professional realm, I'm most grateful for our beautiful friendship. Here's to many more mountains to climb and celebrating together!

To Molly and Lisa,
Our journey began as strangers, sitting with each other at a table in San Diego, and has since blossomed into a cherished friendship. You've been the best accountability buddies, staying true to our goals, celebrating our successes, and navigating the challenges. You've been an invaluable source of motivation and support. I'm forever grateful for you.

To Ashley,
Thank you for bringing my vision to life through your incredible talent and work. You truly are amazing and your photography connects my mission and heart to the world.

To My Support and Self Care Team,
Becki, Molly, Jennifer, Lauren, Tracey, Robin, Ashlyn, & Taylor: You've shown me that self care is allowing myself to lean on the incredible talent each of you have. Thank you for reminding me I don't have to do anything alone.

To My First Aid Team,
Sarah, Ed, David, Michelle, Kristine, Molly, Marjie, Gillian, Devon, and Lezlee:
After I ripped the band-aid off, you were there - ready to help stop the bleeding, repair, and heal. You helped me see a new path, one with fewer roadblocks, and equipped me with the knowledge and confidence to keep moving forward. Thank you from the bottom of my heart for your expertise, passion in your work and getting this book out into the world.

To The Thought Leader Academy and My TLA Pod Sisters,
Your insightful reflections and invaluable guidance provided nourishing enrichment to this writing journey. Thank you for contributing your wisdom and shared experiences. I appreciate your friendship and the shared community that inspires me to keep taking the next step.

To My Beta Readers and Launch Team,
I appreciate your ability to see the nuances that could enrich the narrative and support the "It's Your Turn" mission. I'm so grateful for your unwavering encouragement and the gift of your time to help with my passion project.

To Wendy and Madison of CharlieMadison Originals,
Thank you for creating the beautiful *It's Your Turn* Bracelet. This bracelet perfectly captures the heart of what this journey and book are all about. I'm so grateful for your thoughtful creation.

To Chris, Laura, Nicole, Jana, Debbie, Liz, Michelle, and Sarah,
You remind me every day of the importance of having a coach. You've each taught me so much by sharing your wisdom and expertise in your area of coaching. My investment in community, accountability, and support has helped me go further faster in my life and my business. Thank you for reminding me to keep serving from my heart.

To My Dear Extended Family and Friends,
You know who you are—there are too many to name. You've been the first to cheer in moments of celebration and, in times of challenge, your unwavering support has been a lifeline. You have enriched my life in immeasurable ways. Thank you for your love, kindness, and support.

To My Beloved Mom and Dad and Kathy,
Your unwavering love and enduring support have been the pillars of my life. Your guidance, sacrifices, and countless lessons in compassion have shaped me into the person I am today, and I am profoundly thankful for you.

To My Amazing Son, Kyle,
Your wisdom and selflessness have been a guiding light. Thank you for assisting with editing tasks, cooking dinner, grabbing groceries, and holding down the fort at home. Your support has allowed me the space and time to pour my heart into this book and my business. You're a kind and caring man. Keep reaching for your dreams!

To My Beautiful Daughter, Kaitlyn,
Your insights have been invaluable, and our conversations have been richer by the day. You've reminded me that the purpose behind my mission is to set a better example, showing the next generation of women that prioritizing self-care can have a profound impact on our lives, especially for those we love. You are an incredible woman. Keep making the world a better place!

To My Incredible Husband, John,
You are my rock and unwavering support in life. Thank you for being my biggest encourager and patiently listening to countless "audio versions" of my manuscript. Your belief in me fuels my determination. I'm grateful to have you by my side. Home is where we are together. My heart is filled with so much love for you, Kyle, and Kaitlyn. Let's keep having fun and taking our turn together.

About the Author

S hari Biery, author, speaker, coach, and founder of Alive With Purpose Health & Life Coaching, empowers midlife women through transformative journeys of self-discovery and personal growth.

She holds a bachelor's degree in Business Management and an associate degree in Respiratory Therapy, where she began her career as a registered respiratory therapist and developed a deep passion for empowering and educating patients about their health.

Through frequent relocations and the chaotic lifestyle of military family life, Shari learned valuable lessons on adapting and thriving in stressful circumstances, demonstrating dependable leadership and a sunny personality.

As a military spouse, she navigated a diverse and "curvy" employment journey, working in various industries, including not-for-profit, the private sector, and the federal government. Her roles included registered respiratory therapist, "professional" volunteer, administrative assistant, financial analyst, and project coordinator.

After her husband's military retirement, Shari founded Alive With Purpose Health & Life Coaching after achieving the highest National Board Certified Health and Wellness Coach credential. This certification reflects a National Standard developed by the American Medical Association and the National Board for Health and Wellness Coaches.

Since 2019, Shari has supported hundreds of women in saying "YES" to themselves (often for the first time) and shown them how to design a life plan with intention, awareness, and purpose. Shari also guides midlife women with high-achieving partners to rediscover themselves and prioritize their well-being.

When she's not coaching, speaking, and empowering women, Shari enjoys long walks in nature, traveling, and spending quality time with family and friends.

Learn more about Shari and how you can reclaim your life and well-being by saying *It's My Turn* at sharibiery.com.

I'd Love Your Feedback.
I hope *It's Your Turn* has inspired you to say "yes" to yourself in new ways. If you found the book helpful, I would truly appreciate it if you could leave a quick review on Amazon. Your feedback will help other women looking to make positive changes in their lives. It doesn't have to be long or detailed—just a few sentences about what resonated with you can make a big difference.

How to Leave a Review on Amazon:
Simply go to the book's product page and click on the "Write a Review" button. After providing your information, you can add a rating and a brief review of the book, describing what you found helpful and what you learned.

Here are a few things you can mention in your review:
What did you find most helpful about the book?
What did you learn that you didn't know before?
Why would you recommend this book to others?

Endnotes

Chapter 2

1. Michelle Obama, *Becoming* (New York: Crown, 2021).

2. Laura Bush, *Spoken from the Heart* (Waterville, Me: Thorndike Press, 2010).

3. Blue Star Families, "Military Family Lifestyle Survey Results 2021: Comprehensive Report," March 14, 2022, https://bluestarfam.org/wp-content/uploads/2022/03/BSF_MFLS_Results2021_ComprehensiveReport_03_14.pdf

4. "Roadmap to Employment Stability for Military Spouses. Five Recommendations to Build Financial Security throughout the Military Lifecycle," 2021, https://www.nationalmilitaryspousenetwork.org/public/images/2021_White_Paper_NMSN.pdf. Accessed 2023.

5. "Solving the Military Spouse Employment Puzzle: Seven Recommendations for the Future of Work," 2023, https://www.nationalmilitaryspousenetwork.org/public/images/2023_NMSN_White_Paper.pdf. Accessed 2023

6. "Executive Order on Advancing Economic Security for Military and Veteran Spouses, Military Caregivers, and Survivors," Washington, DC, June 9, 2023, https://www.whitehouse.gov/briefing-room/presidential-actions/202

3/06/09/executive-order-on-advancing-economic-security-for-military-and-veteran-spouses-military-caregivers-and-survivors/. Accessed 2023.

7. Glennon Doyle, *Untamed* (New York: Random House, 2020), 332.

8. "Women @ Work 2023: A Global Outlook," 2023, https://www.deloitte.com/global/en/issues/work/content/women-at-work-global-outlook.html. Accessed 2023.

9. "American Time Use Survey–2022 Results," 2023, https://www.bls.gov/news.release/pdf/atus.pdf. Accessed 2023.

10. Allison Daminger, "The Cognitive Dimension of Household Labor," July 9, 2019, https://doi.org/10.1177/0003122419859007. Accessed 2023.

11. "Burn-out an 'Occupational Phenomenon': International Classification of Diseases," May 28, 2019, https://www.who.int/news/item/28-05-2019-burn-out-an-occupational-phenomenon-international-classification-of-diseases. Accessed 2023.

12. Brené Brown, *Atlas of the Heart* (New York: Random House, November 2021), 31-33.

Chapter 4

1. "Compassionate Integrity Training," https://www.compassionateintegrity.org/#. Accessed 2023.

2. "VIA Institute on Character," https://www.viacharacter.org. Accessed 2023.

Chapter 5

1. "Procrastination," 2023, https://www.psychologytoday
   .com/us/basics/procrastination#understanding-
   procrastination. Accessed 2023.

Chapter 6

1. Anna Medaris, "Women Say They're Stressed,
   Misunderstood, and Alone," November 1, 2023, https:
   //www.apa.org/topics/stress/women-stress. Accessed
   2023.

2. "About Chronic Diseases," July 21, 2022,
   https://www.cdc.gov/chronicdisease/about/index.htm.
   Accessed 2023.

3. "Healthy Habits Can Lengthen Life," May 8, 2018,
   https://www.nih.gov/news-events/nih-research-matters/
   healthy-habits-can-lengthen-life. Accessed 2023.

4. "Why Most New Year's Resolutions Fail," February 2, 2023
   https://fisher.osu.edu/blogs/leadreadtoday/why-most-n
   ew-years-resolutions-fail#:~:text=Researchers%20sugge
   st%20that%20only%209,fail%20at%20New%20Year%27
   s%20resolutions. Accessed 2023.

5. Emily Nagoski and Amelia Nagoski, *Burnout: The Secret
   to Unlocking the Stress Cycle* (New York: Ballantine Books,
   2019), 14-21.

6. "Cortisol," 2023, https://my.clevelandclinic.org/health
   /articles/22187-cortisol. Accessed 2023.

7. "How Stress Affects Your Health," October 31, 2022, https:
   //www.apa.org/topics/stress/health. Accessed 2023.

8. Cleveland Clinic, "Insulin Resistance," Cleveland, Ohio, 2024, https://my.clevelandclinic.org/health/diseases /22206-insulin-resistance. Accessed 2023.

9. Molly McGrath, *"Answering Your Craving for Rest,"* February 13, 2023, https://hiringandempowering.com /answering-your-craving-for-rest/. Accessed 2023.

10. James Clear, *Atomic Habits: Tiny Changes, Remarkable Results: An Easy & Proven Way to Build Good Habits & Break Bad Ones* (New York: Penguin Random House, October 16, 2018), 108-111.

11. "Stress in America 2023: A Nation Recovering from Collective Trauma," 2023, https://www.apa.org/news /press/releases/stress/2023/collective-trauma-recovery. Accessed 2023.

12. "Our Epidemic of Loneliness and Isolation," 2023, https://www.hhs.gov/sites/default/files/surgeon-general -social-connection-advisory.pdf. Accessed 2023.

13. Jones, Blake L., Adam L. Orton, Spencer W. Tindall, Joshua T. Christensen, Osayamen Enosakhare, Keeley A. Russell, Anne-Marie Robins, Ana Larriviere-McCarl, Joseph Sandres, Braden Cox, and et al. 2023. "Barriers to Healthy Family Dinners and Preventing Child Obesity: Focus Group Discussions with Parents of 5-to-8-Year-Old Children," *Children* 10, no. 6: 952. https://doi.org/10.3390/children10060952. Accessed 2023.

14. Mark Hyman, "Food Is Medicine: How Doctors Can Prescribe Food For Chronic Disease," August 30, 2023, https://drhyman.com/blog/2023/08/30/podcast-ep772/ #:~:text=Walker%3A%20That%27s%20right.-,Dr.,can%27

t%20do%20with%20drugs. Accessed 2023.

15. "Sleep and Sleep Disorders," September 7, 2022, https://www.cdc.gov/sleep/index.html. Accessed 2023.

Chapter 7

1. "Girls on the Run," 2023, https://www. girlsontherun.org. Accessed 2023.

2. "Healthy Brains," 2022, https://healthybrains.org/brain-facts/. Accessed 2023.

3. Kendra Cherry, *"Biography of Psychologist Albert Ellis,"* July 27, 2023, https://www.verywellmind.com /albert-ellis-biography-2795493. Accessed 2023.

4. Scott Frothingham, "What is Negativity Bias, and How Does it Affect You?" December 17, 2019, https://www. healthline.com/health/negativity-bias. Accessed 2023.

5. "Neuroplasticity," 2023, https://www.psychologytoday .com/us/basics/neuroplasticity. Accessed 2023.

6. "Self-Love Crisis: 1 in 2 Women Worldwide Feel More Self-doubt Than Self-love" March 8, 2021, https://www. prnewswire.com/news-releases/self-love-crisis-1-in-2-w omen-worldwide-feel-more-self-doubt-than-self-love-30 1241851.html. Accessed 2023.

7. Bruce Lipton, *The Biology of Belief: Unleashing the Power of Consciousness, Matter and Miracles* (Carlsbad, CA: Hay House, Inc., 2005).

www.ingramcontent.com/pod-product-compliance
Lightning Source LLC
Chambersburg PA
CBHW060759120626
46557CB00001B/35